THE NO HOPER

Schoolboy howlers from the 1940s

by David Skentelbery

For Patricia
*(who is convinced I went to some
form of institution for backward boys)*

ORBIT PUBLISHING, WARRINGTON

THE NO HOPER

Copyright © 2021 David Skentelbery All rights reserved

No part of this book may be reproduced, or stored in a retrieval system, or transmitted in any form or by any means, electronic, mechanical, photocopying, recording, or otherwise, without express written permission of the publisher.

ISBN-9798599191971

Cover: The Delamere Runner, from paintings by Hannah Skentelbery and John Samples

THE NO HOPER

PREFACE

I should have written this book years ago. Not because it is an important but neglected piece of Cheshire history, although it could be argued that it is. Not because it casts a critical eye on mid-20th century independent education, although it does. But simply because it's a bloody funny story.

Tom Brown's Schooldays it is not. Neither is it Billy Bunter of Greyfriars School. There is no Flashman stalking its pages, no Fat Owl of the Remove, no Mr Quelch. But the characters who attended Knutsford College between 1927 and 1954 were many and varied and just as colourful. More importantly they were real, for this is not a work of fiction. The events described, unbelievable as some are, really happened.

Some names are omitted to protect the innocent. Others to protect the guilty. A few because I can't remember who the hell they were.

It cannot be described as a history of Knutsford College because I can only write of my time there. But I arrived when it was still in its pomp and I was still there when, sadly, it closed. I have had the advantage of speaking to many who were there before me and of reading the contents of the excellent website www.knutsford-college.com, owned and edited by former student Doug Griffiths.

There are those who suggest Knutsford College could be compared with Dotheboys Hall, the infamous boarding school described by Charles Dickens in Nicholas Nickleby. But I believe it was a character-forming school which, for the most part, turned out young men who made the most of the rest of their lives. Sadly, many have passed on, but among the survivors you will be hard pressed to find any who are not proud to be Old Boys of Knutsford College.

The No Hoper

THE NO HOPER

It would put Charles Dickens and "Dotheboys Hall" to shame – Peter Chadwick, former student at Knutsford College

THE NO HOPER

IN THE BEGINNING

Early morning sunlight filtered through the cedar trees. The sky was a cloudless blue. The air smelled fresh and clean. It would have been beautiful but for one thing. It was my first day at a new school and I was wishing I was somewhere else – anywhere else.

The cedar trees formed an avenue along which a squad of young boys marched, heads held high, shoulders back, arms swinging. Three columns of youngsters, moving like a well-oiled machine along the drive towards the elegant, Gothic style mock Tudor mansion which dominated the scene.

"Left, left, left, right, left."

A senior boy ensured the squad kept moving with a staccato cry. The whole object was to keep the boys moving, not as individuals, but as a single entity. Each boy marched with a measured stride, his arms swinging to exactly shoulder height. Most were clad in grey, either shorts or flannels. Most wore black shoes. This was precision stuff.

Yet one boy stood out. Tall, handsome, tanned and athletic in build. His every move suggested confidence. A born leader if ever there was one.

No it wasn't me. In fact, looking back or looking around the gatherings at recent Old Boy's reunions, I can't think who the hell it could have been!

I'm the one at the back. The chubby one, with freckles, a big round face and untidy hair, out-of-step and wearing not grey but a full length, belted, navy blue raincoat and with a school satchel bouncing up and down on my back.

The year was 1948 and this was Knutsford College, a boarding school for the sons of gentlemen in Cheshire, Motto: "Spes anchora vitae" - "Hope - the Anchor of Life".

An impressive motto, you might think. Until you learn the school was run by a man named Hope.

That sunny morning marked the start of the first day of a new term. My first term.

THE NO HOPER

But before we go deeper into that first morning and why I was so unsuitably clad for the military-style drill which marked the start of each day at this establishment of learning, let me explain how I, a child of Hitler's blitz, the extremely shy son of that rare individual, a shy journalist, came to be there at all.

It was some eight years earlier that I had arrived in Knutsford, famed as the town on which the Victorian authoress Elizabeth Cleghorn Gaskell had based her novel "Cranford". I came in the back of a van and was wearing women's underwear at the time
What's that, I hear you say? Women's underwear? Nothing much shy about you, then!
Let me clarify that point. My parents and I were victims of the blitzkrieg which Germany's Luftwaffe launched on Manchester just before the Christmas of 1940. Our house, in what was then, I am told, the leafy suburb of Whalley Range, was devastated by two bombs which fell in the garden. I was, in fact, lucky to be alive.
I have said my father was shy, and so he was. But he must also have been a man of some considerable courage.
You don't grow up thinking of your father being brave, do you? Or at least I didn't.
But on that night in December, 1940 he must have been extremely brave.
My mother had gone to Liverpool, also suffering the attentions of the Luftwaffe, to spend a few days with her mother, so Dad, his own mother and I were left in Whalley Range and as the German bombers droned overhead through a sky illuminated by searchlights and bursting anti-aircraft shells, my Grandma and I cowered under the stairs. At least she did - I was fast asleep. It takes more than a bombing raid to keep me awake, I can tell you.
Dad was an Air Raid Warden and was probably out in the street shouting "Put that light out."

THE NO HOPER

The first bomb to fall in our garden shook the house to its foundations and probably left it uninhabitable. I can't be sure about this because, for one thing, I was only three and for another, I was still asleep.

Dad apparently arrived back at the house to find it in ruins and realised it had to be evacuated before it fell in on us. He dragged me out from under the stairs and laid me on a settee while he went back to help my Grandma.

I did mention she was disabled, didn't I? No? Well, some years previously she had fractured her femur in a fall and, in those days, that often meant you were crippled for life. She could only walk with the aid of two crutches.

Dad faced the problem of getting the two of us to the nearest air raid shelter. He could run with me in his arms but if Grandma accompanied us we would have to walk at her pace.

He was trying to make up his mind who to take first when the second bomb came down.

The blast blew a heavy patio door from its hinges and sent it hurtling across the living room to where I still slept blissfully on the settee. It would have certainly hit me if my mother's grand piano had not stood between the window and the settee.

The piano - ironically made in Germany by one Emile Leuttner - took the full blast, almost certainly saving my life.

Dad made his decision. He would take me first and then return for his mother, who was still sheltering under what was left of the stairs

He ran through streets littered with slates, dislodged bricks, chunks of masonry and shattered chimney pots, carrying me. Still asleep, I assure you!

It must have been terrifying because the raid was still going on. German bombers still droned overhead, the ground was shaking as bombs exploded to the left and to the right. The sky was rent by bursting anti-aircraft shells. Somehow he got me to the shelter, already packed with local people whose homes might, or might not, have also been wrecked. He spotted a family he knew slightly - a mother and her two daughters in their twenties - and left me with them. Then it was back to the house to make the perilous journey again. This time at his mother's pace.

So, yes, my father proved himself a brave man that night, just as I proved myself a sound sleeper. When the raid was over, the mother and two daughters showed the friendship which flourished among people during the Blitz by taking us back to their home for the rest of the night and, with all my clothing lost, dressing me in one of the girls' underwear.

Our next door neighbours, George and Nancy Wildsmith, had lost their home too and, next morning, as they and Dad stood together, surveying the damage, George and Nan showed my father the sort of neighbourliness that was to make them my parents' closest friends for the rest of their lives.

George said: "Nan's mother lives at Knutsford. We're going there - you must come with us."

That evening, when my mother arrived home after a tortuous all-day journey by various trains and buses still keeping open some sort of service between Liverpool and Manchester, she found a note pinned to the shattered front door of our wrecked house. It read, simply: "Gone to Knutsford. All well."

I, by this time had arrived in the town which was to be my home for the next 20 or so years. Still wearing a young woman's underwear.

So, back to school. Not Knutsford College yet, but an independent primary school, Yorston Lodge, which still flourishes today in the same buildings it occupied then, at the corner of Bexton Road and St John's Avenue.

I have few memories of life at Yorston Lodge. It was then run by three sisters - Miss Nan, Miss Daisy and the stern headmistress who was simply known as Miss Brydon. In fact, the school was better known as "Miss Brydon's" than by its real name.

I recall being something of a duffer at maths and being sternly reminded by Miss Nan that the word "water" had a "T" in the middle. I remember getting stuck in the loo one day and taking so long to extricate myself that when I emerged I was confronted by a long queue of little girls literally dancing in pools of water.

Then there was the day the school bully picked on me and I displayed, for the first time in my life, the temper which occasionally over the subsequent years, has burst out uncontrollably. I laid him out on the cloakroom floor. Of course, he gave me a good hiding the following day when my temper was so conspicuous by its absence that I just let him hit me again and again.

Yorston Lodge was, I suppose, quite a genteel school. But that did not prevent outbursts of ribald humour, certainly among the boys. The War was still on, of course, which meant the target of much of this humour was Mr Hitler and his cronies. It was all a bit over my head – for instance when I heard a crude rhyme about Hitler and Goering "throwing away their guns and using their dicks instead" I went home and repeated it to my shocked mother.

When I got a telling off I innocently protested that the word "dicks" meant "dicky birds" – and really believed it did.

I don't know if, by this time, I retained any memories of being bombed out in the Manchester blitz, but I suspect not. After all, I had slept through most of it, as you will recall. In Knutsford, you would hardly have known there was a war on – at least not until the US Army arrived and set up camp on The Heath in readiness for D Day.

But a couple of things did happen to make me aware of the conflict. One, my Dad, was called up by the RAF, despite being aged over 40. I remember crying at the thought that he might be shot down while flying his Spitfire. It took him some time to convince me that he would not actually be flying an aeroplane and would be safe. Neither of us knew, of course, that he would be discharged on health grounds nine months later, before the war had ended.

THE NO HOPER

The other was that for a time we had an evacuee staying with us. He was a cocky little Londoner named Derek who was as streetwise as I was shy. What he thought of me I shudder to think, but for a while he became almost a "brother" and we got on pretty well.
He called my Mum "auntie" and one day he came running in from the garden shouting "Auntie, auntie – a doodlebug is coming."
My Mum said: "Don't be silly Derek – we don't get doodlebugs here."
But the lad was right. He'd heard them before, at home in London.
The following day we heard that a stray V1 rocket had crashed in a nearby field. My Mum took us a walk to see it but the area had been sealed off by the police so we couldn't get near it.
I remember being off school and in hospital for a month with Scarlet Fever. I think the War must have been over by then or I wouldn't have been sent from the comparative safety of Knutsford to Monsal Hospital, in Manchester. It was an isolation hospital, which meant your visitors could only see you through glass doors at the end of a long ward, filled with beds containing sick children. I used to wave frantically to my Mum from my bed, which was so far away from the door that I could never be quite sure it was my Mum I was waving to.
Two other memories I have of my first school perhaps give an indication of what a pathetic creature I was.
One was the day I was in the school grounds, idling around watching some little girls play tennis and, it seemed to me, to be doing their best to break a window or two.
Suddenly I heard a loud man's voice, booming in the distance but rapidly getting nearer and louder. My immediate thought was that Knutsford had been invaded by some monstrous giant who had already destroyed the town and was now heading for Yorston Lodge.
I fled inside the school seeking protection from Miss Nan or Miss Daisy – only to discover it was not a giant heading our way but a loudspeaker van broadcasting an election day message.
The other was when the Knutsford area was to receive a Royal visit.

THE NO HOPER

Arrangements were made for our school to stand at a particular point from which we would be able to see the procession of Royal cars sweeping majestically by. We were all issued with flags and given instructions on how, in the case of boys, to bow and the case of girls, to curtsy.

I think the visit was by the King and Queen but I can't be sure because I was too busy bowing to get more than a brief glimpse of a big, shiny black car, while everyone else was jumping up and down, cheering and waving their flags, having apparently forgotten all about the instructions to bow and curtsy.

But the main thing I remember about Yorston Lodge was the introduction Miss Nan and Miss Daisy gave me to the sport that has remained with me for the rest of the my life. Cricket.

In those days the school had the use of what was known as "The Station Field." It's a row of bungalows in St John's Road, backing on to the railway now, but then it was a long, narrow strip of green separating the houses on the other side of the road from the railway. There, we played cricket once a week in the summer.

In later years the Yorkshire and England fast bowler-turned radio pundit Fred Trueman would become famous for his oft repeated dictum that cricket is "a sideways game." Miss Nan and Miss Daisy knew that before he was born. I was taught to adopt a sideways position to bat and to bowl. I was reluctant to accept this advice as, like most other young would-be cricketers, I wanted to take a 30-yard run and hurl the ball at the batsman - or possibly batswoman when you were at Yorston Lodge - with all my might, irrespective of whether I was sideways on. Fred Trueman and I later learned that the Misses Brydon were right - although I assume he received the information elsewhere.

My shyness almost vanished on the cricket field. This was something I was good at - better than most of my contemporaries. And it was cricket that was to prove my saviour some years later when my parents, apparently by now believing their shy son was something of a "No Hoper"

decided he would have an easier journey through secondary education at an independent school than at the local state school.
Little did they know.

THE FIRST DAY

We have seen already that Dad was a brave man and a caring one. I have also said he was shy, although even that should be qualified. He was for much of his journalistic career a drama critic and frequently had to present trophies to award-winning actors and actresses. Put him in a black tie and evening suit and he could stand on a stage and hold an audience's attention for what seemed to me, when I was in that audience, an interminable age.

But for ordinary, day-to-day living, he was, without doubt, shy. He made the decision early on in his career that the life of a reporter, pushing his way into other people's lives at times when they often wanted to be left alone, was not for him. So he became a sub-editor which, in those days, was largely a matter of dotting Is, crossing Ts and correcting other people's spelling mistakes and grammar. Would that I had him now!

So, yes, he was shy and it was probably his shyness that made me late for my first day at Knutsford College.

We had been there before, of course. For the interview. Mum and Dad and I had walked together the half mile or so from our home in Stanley Road, down Adams Hill, up Hollow Lane, along Thorneyholme Drive and up the impressive tree-lined drive to the even more impressive mansion that housed the college. I can remember little about the interview with Mr E.P. Hope except that he impressed me with his gown, which bore some form of military-style insignia.

E.P., or "Percy" as I and everyone else at Knutsford College came to call him behind his back, did most of the talking, I think. Dad had his say and Mum made a few contributions. I just sat there.

Afterwards, as word began to spread among my parents' circle of friends and acquaintances, that I was to be sent to Knutsford College, I recall conversations between Mum and other boys' mothers in which I would hear her say in a slightly affected accent: "Oh no, there is no entrance examination. It is based on an interview."

THE NO HOPER

At the time this meant little to me but in later years I have wondered whether the interview had very little to do with my academic ability and suitability for the school, but rather more to do with Percy satisfying himself that my parents had the ability to pay.

My father took a morning off work to walk me to school on my first day. Whatever world-shattering news was breaking and whatever pressures it caused at the Manchester Evening Chronicle, it took second place to my first day at a new school. They had to manage without Dad.

Looking back, I should feel extremely flattered that he was prepared to take time off for me. Shy he may have been but he was also a workaholic with a strong sense of vocation and would not lightly have decided that I needed his support. Perhaps it is an indication of just how timid a creature I was.

The walk seemed much longer than when we had gone for the interview and I am not sure who dragged their feet the most, me or Dad. We talked and I imagine he was giving me fatherly advice on how to handle myself with other pupils. Perhaps he gave me good advice, perhaps not. I suspect I was so terrified that it simply went in one ear and out the other. Anyway. I certainly have no recollection of what was said.

But I have vivid memories of our eventual arrival - probably 15 minutes late. Dad took me to the front door, as on our earlier visit, neither of us knowing that the normal route into school for pupils was through an archway, into a cobbled courtyard and from thence round the back of the building to another entrance, next to the cloakroom. Dad rang the bell and we stood, nervously waiting, for a considerable time before the door was eventually opened by a woman who I later learned was Brenda.

Brenda Mewter was, I think, a member of the school's domestic staff during the whole of my time at Knutsford College. During school hours, she was one of the few members of the opposite sex we boys came into contact with. I am pretty sure she was the only one less than 30. She did, I

THE NO HOPER

believe, attract some admiration from some of my older schoolmates, but to me she was, simply, Brenda.

Now what Brenda should have done that morning was take me to the cloakroom, where I could have left my navy blue, belted raincoat and my leather satchel. She should then have taken me along the cedar drive to the cricket field, where drill was taking place, and handed me over to one of the supervising teachers. In fact, she took me straight to the field, raincoat, satchel and all.

A perplexed master - I can't remember who – wasn't quite sure what to do with me but told me to "fall in" at the back of a squad of boys of about my age. I think the drill session must have been drawing to a close as I have no recollection of doing anything other than marching back along the cedar drive to the main building.

One or two rather amused boys stared at me, obviously puzzled by this newcomer so unsuitably attired for the drill squad.

One boy, small, fair-haired, probably little more than half my height but from his confident demeanour, seeming to tower above me, stared me in the face.

"What's your name, then?"

"Er...David."

"We don't use first names here. What's your surname?"

"Er...Skentelbery."

"What'll berry?"

"Er, Skentelbery."

"Skentel WHAT?'

I fell silent, unable to think of what else to say.

He regarded me for a few moments, uncertain whether to ridicule me further or to take pity on me. Eventually he must have decided to do both.

"Well, Skentel-bollocks, I'd better show you where the cloakroom is."

I think that was what he did, but most of that time has been mercifully blanked from my memory. I'm still embarrassed by it now, a life time later.

THE NO HOPER

The rest of that first day may have been equally embarrassing because I can't remember much about it except assembly and roll call and lunch.

Assembly, which comprised of hymn singing, prayers and roll-call was held in the largest classroom. On the first day of term there were always new boys and if they had unusual surnames this caused great hilarity at roll-call. Sometimes it would be a suppressed snicker from a few, sometimes outright laughter from many. When my name "Skentelbery" was called out, the entire school appeared to me to collapse with uncontrollable laughter.

The classroom where Assembly took place

I wanted the ground to open and swallow me up. I mean, didn't they know that Skentelbery was an ancient, occupational name that could be traced back to Cornwall in 1515 and probably indicated my forebears were skilled craftsmen? Did they not know it was believed there had once been a Lord Skentelbery? And what about the Thomas Skentelbery who was an Indian fighter who served in the U.S. Seventh Cavalry under General Custer and survived the Battle of Little Big Horn by the simple ruse of not being there that day?

Why hadn't the wretched man been there? If he had been, perhaps I wouldn't have been here today, I thought. Or if I was, perhaps I would have been called Smith or Brown.

But no, they didn't know any of this. To them, my name was just one huge joke.

The whole, horrible affair led to "Skentelbollocks" becoming my nickname for some time. It was a name that I eventually lived down and even managed to forget – until my good friend and former classmate John

THE NO HOPER

White was kind enough to pass it on to my son, Gary, when he was in his teens!

Over the years, other new boys with unusual names suffered similar fates at Knutsford College and I probably laughed at their discomfort as much as anyone. It is only in later years that the value of an unusual name sometimes becomes apparent.

But I said I remembered lunch on that first day too. Yes - again with some embarrassment.

It seemed to me that everyone knew instinctively what to do and where to go next. Everybody except me, that is. I'm sure there were other new boys that day, but if there were I had no idea who they were. I could not join with them and form some sort of group that would have given some protection from the great mass of streetwise youngsters who knew everything there was to know but were apparently unwilling to share their knowledge and experience.

So when lunchtime came I was the last in the dining room. I have no idea how I got to the dining room at all but I suppose someone most have taken sufficient pity on me to point me in the right direction. I have a recollection of a mad rush for chairs, the scraping of wooden chair legs on a polished wooden floor and a clamour of voices claiming places at particular tables. When silence eventually fell I was left dejectedly standing in the middle of the room with nowhere to sit.

A master said Grace and with another scraping of chair legs on wood, everyone sat down and the master at last noticed that he had one boy stranded without a seat. I seem to recall an awkward few moments while he decided what to do with me.

There appeared to be only one table with an empty chair and that was one occupied by about five senior boys who, to me, seemed like fully grown men. I was instructed to join this elite group and, in fairness, the five of them welcomed me and did their best to make me feel at ease. But I could not really join in their conversation and they talked to me rather in the manner of someone addressing a puppy.

THE NO HOPER

Again, my memories of that first meal at Knutsford College have been mercifully erased from my mind. But I do remember that for some weeks, if not months, I remained at that table with the same five young men. One, I recall, shocked the other four by the amount of salt he would add to his dinner - almost half a salt pot with every meal.

About once a week we used to have for dessert, a sort of steamed suet pudding, over which was poured in those ration-book post war days, a sauce which appeared to consist of melted raspberry jam diluted by hot water. One of my companions hated it and referred it as "rainwater." I quite liked it though and he invariably gave me his portion.

No wonder I was considered chubby by my classmates.

THE INITIATION CEREMONY

Somehow or other, on my first day at Knutsford College, I managed to avoid the initiation ceremony. On my second day, I was not so fortunate.

There are many among my contemporaries who, in later life, profess to having no recollection of any initiation ceremony. This could, of course, be a manifestation of that curse of later life, the failing memory. On the other hand, it could be a "convenient" loss of memory, brought about by a sense of embarrassment at the prospect of having to reveal all in front of an audience of former school pals.

A third, and entirely likely, possibility is that only new boys of a somewhat timid and retiring nature were subjected to any such ordeal. Given my inauspicious start at the school I would clearly have been marked down as a suitable candidate.

So far as I can recall, I committed no serious errors on my second day. I arrived on time and assembled with my classmates for drill. I now knew, of course, that I was in Class 2B, so there was no problem there.

I should, perhaps, at this stage, break off briefly to explain that due to its modest size, Knutsford College had only four classes. For some reason they were known as Third Class, 2B, 2A and First Class. Age, rather than educational attainment, was used to decide which class you were placed in, although I believe brighter boys were occasionally promoted in advance of their birthday. My only recollection of advancement through the ranks was that on two occasions I was suddenly informed, part way through the school day, that I was being moved up and had to empty my desk of my possessions and scurry to the next room. As on neither occasion did the move seem to coincide with a birthday, I suspect it had more to do with a shortage of desks in one class or a surplus of them in another.

Third Class was for boys of primary school age and was, as far as I can recall, always during my time at the school, taught by a woman. The only one I can remember was Miss Dick who, quite remarkably, managed to

THE NO HOPER

avoid the sort of coarse humour that her name would probably provoke today. I avoided Third Class by virtue of having received my early education from the Misses Brydon.
So there I was with my classmates from 2B, reporting promptly for drill on my second day, this time without being encumbered with a satchel and raincoat.
Drill was not something I found particularly enjoyable. All the bending and touching your toes, the jumping and clapping your hands above you r head, the muscle wrenching arm exercises. It was all a bit much at nine o'clock in the morning. And then there was the marching, sometimes at the double. If you were lucky, the senior boy in charge of your squad would simply march you round the cricket field a few times. If you were not so lucky the march could take you down Manor Park Drive, as far as the Post Office in Cross Town, where the squad would come under the curious gaze of the local population.
Anyway, drill on that second day does not stick in my memory as being any different to any other day. It preceded the morning lessons and, of course, the lunchtime break. It also preceded the initiation ceremony.
Who they were and how they lured me to the relative isolation of the cricket field I cannot recall. But somehow, I ended up there, surrounded by a group of more worldly wise boys.
It was all very civilised. I was told what was going to happen and why. I was to be thrown, head first into a large holly bush which stood at the edge of the field. After that, I was assured, I would be accepted as one of the gang.
Whether I acquiesced and allowed myself to be flung into the bush, or whether I had to be dragged screaming and shouting, I cannot say. But I can recall being swung back and to by four boys, each holding me by a leg or an arm, and eventually being released so that I flew through the air, in a gentle arc, to crash headlong into the prickly bush. Ouch!

THE NO HOPER

I don't recall that the ordeal did, in fact, enable me to become "one of the gang." I suspect it did not, for I endured various other hardships over the coming months which are too embarrassing even to recall.

You see, it was the wrong time of year – football was the main topic of conversation between lessons, the sole organised sport in the school, and I did not like football – nor know anything about it.

It soon became obvious to me that it would be advantageous to become a football fan and to support a particular team. Nearly everyone seemed to support Manchester United but, even at that age, I had developed an awkward streak which made me want to be different.

I went home and asked my Dad, who was himself a Manchester United fan, which team I should support. He pointed out that we had only moved to Manchester a few months before the start of the war and that prior to that we had lived in Birmingham, where I had been born. I should support the city of my birth, he said, which meant I could support either Birmingham City or Aston Villa.

At that time, Aston Villa were one of the leading clubs in the country and had won the FA Cup more times than any other club. Displaying my usual talent for making wrong decisions, I decided to become a Birmingham supporter.

Far from gaining me some much needed kudos among my school mates it simply exposed me to more ridicule because Birmingham then, and indeed now, never seemed to win anything. Even today when they occasionally get promoted to the top flight it always seems to be as runners-up – and usually they are heading down again pretty quickly. So football remained a topic of little interest to me.

The school cricket field at this time of the year was only in use for drill, initiation ceremonies and as a secluded place for some pupils to smoke cigarettes they had probably stolen from their parents. So it was some time before the summer game became a subject of conversation and it was only then that I was able to suddenly command some respect. For I was a member of Knutsford Cricket Club's junior section. I don't recall how it

THE NO HOPER

started, but somehow cricket cropped up in a conversation among a group of pupils of varying ages to which I had attached myself. A boy some years older than I, suddenly turned to me and said: "Skentelbollocks - can you play cricket? He was probably expecting an answer in the negative, or perhaps even an admission that I didn't know what cricket was.

But in fact I replied: "Yes – I'm a member of Knutsford Juniors."

There was a stunned silence. Six or seven pairs of eyes widened and swung in my direction. Six or seven faces moved closer to mine, bearing expressions ranging from incredulity to frank disbelief.

"You - you are a member of Knutsford Juniors?"

"Er..yes. I have been for a couple of years."

Looking back, it surprises me that being a junior member of Knutsford Cricket Club carried any sway among my fellow pupils. But it did - and I found myself immediately being cross-examined in great detail about my experiences as a member of Knutsford Juniors. I can't remember what I told them, but my standing in the school rose so much from that moment on that I can only assume that I relied heavily on my imagination.

Knutsford Cricket Club played then, as now, in Mere Heath Lane. Organised sport in Britain had, at the grass roots level anyway, been disrupted by Mr Hitler's War and took many years to recover, so at this time, Knutsford did not play in a league but instead played "friendly" matches against other clubs in the Cheshire and South Manchester areas.

My claim to being a member of Knutsford Juniors was based solely on my father taking me down to the ground two or three times to net practice, having a word with some of the players and arranging for me to be coached by the club coach, one Jack Tipping, who, we were assured, was a former Lancashire player.

His coaching mainly consisted of extolling the virtues of "the straight bat" and hurling a corky ball at me from a distance of only a couple of yards to show me how to play it.

Mr Tipping, in addition to being the club coach, also played for the 1st XI and I went on many occasions, accompanied by my father, to see them

THE NO HOPER

perform. We had great expectations of my coach but invariably went home disappointed as he never produced the sort of display we would have expected from a former Lancashire player. I have searched the pages of Wisden Cricketer's Almanac and also the internet but can find no record of a Jack Tipping playing for Lancashire. One piece of advice he gave me was that you should always try to keep the ball on the ground.

Len Hutton doesn't hit sixes, lad," he used to say.

In fact the Yorkshire and England opening batsman, who at that time held the record for the highest score ever hit in a Test match, 364, did occasionally hit sixes. But Mr Tipping's theory that the extra two runs you got for clearing the boundary rope were not worth the risk of being caught is borne out by a study of Hutton's career record. For a batsman who scored 6,971 runs in 79 Test matches, a total of just seven sixes is remarkably low compared with the sloggers who thrive in county and even international cricket today.

I have no recollection of how I went on when the cricket season started and 2B were released into the open air for a full afternoon of the summer game every week. But I must have done

Me - in Jack Tipping mode

reasonably well because I was selected for the school team, in the company of boys mostly several years older than me, when a match was arranged against the local State school, Cross Town School.

Knutsford College boys who travelled to school by bus from Mobberley had to walk passed Cross Town School after alighting from the bus and suffered a daily tirade of abuse from the Cross Towners who considered them to be "posh." It seemed quite unfair to me because whatever shortcomings my school mates had, being "posh" was not one of them.

THE NO HOPER

Anyway, posh or not, we certainly gave them a hammering on the cricket field.

The match was played of an evening and we batted first and scored well over 100, a boy named Don Carter becoming the hero of the whole school with a superb 50.

I remember him hitting a six that clattered through the branches of the mature oak tree that served as a scoreboard in those days. Don had clearly not been coached by Jack Tipping.

I was lucky to get a bat at all, I suppose, and scored seven not out before our innings was declared closed. I suspect I adhered to the Jack Tipping philosophy of a straight bat and keeping the ball on the ground, defending my wicket resolutely as if playing to rescue the team from almost certain defeat. I needn't have bothered because the Cross Town team were dismissed for just three runs - two of which were extras. I don't know who the demon bowlers were, but I wasn't one of them.

A STATELY HOME

Woodside in 1927 - the year it became a school

I wonder how many Knutsford College students, in later life, found themselves being cajoled by wives or partners, into watching Downton Abbey on television?

How many, I wonder, looked contemptuously at Highclere Castle, the ancient pile in Hampshire, which was used to film the series, sniffed and said: "I went to a school like that."

OK, Woodside was a tad smaller, but it was built around the same time and had the advantage of being erected on a virgin site rather than being a refurb of something built on the same piece of land a few hundred years earlier.

Granted, it was owned by a businessman, not an earl, but it could well have had a butler named Carson, because it certainly had a butler's pantry, and Martha Moston,

THE NO HOPER

who reigned supreme in the kitchen, would definitely have given Mrs Patmore a run for her money.

Woodside was a Victorian Mock Tudor mansion, built around 1850 by Henry Long on a 14-acre plot in an area known as Norbury Booths, a historic part of Knutsford that had been inhabited well before the Domesday Book was written.

Henry Long and his wife, Mary, had seven children – all girls – and employed seven servants, so it would have been a pretty busy house.

In 1885, following Mr Long's death, the house was bought by one Charles Galloway, who also bought adjoining land on which he built an even larger house, Thorneyholme, before selling Woodside to Mr Hugh Birley and his wife Amy. They had five children and employed six servants so, again, it would have been pretty lively.

Up until this time it had been known as Woodlands, but its name had been changed to Woodside by the time Percy Hope bought it when he moved his school there in 1927. A number of similar mansions occupied adjoining sites, including Thorneyholme – the largest – Rockford Lodge and Sharston House.

Only Sharston House, the smallest and now a care home, remains.

We students saw Woodside simply as a school and I, for one, spent no time at all pondering what it might have been like when it was a stately home, housing not just a family but a small army of servants as well.

The front of Woodside had a double storied vestibule with ornamental turrets at the upper corners. At the rear was a billiards room – it became the dining room when the college opened - which had a large moulded wainscot around the inner walls and large tracery windows. The east and south sides of the house had a wide terrace from which steps led down to a double line of Cedars of Lebanon that led to the cricket field.

There was a rose garden beneath the terrace with a sundial and large lawns with masses of rhododendrons at each corner. From this there was a pathway through a shrubbery to a summerhouse and then a wood that divided the cricket field from the football field. What these fields were

THE NO HOPER

used for before the school arrived must remain a matter for conjecture, but possibly for grazing horses.

There were two other woods and a large kitchen garden with a greenhouse and potting shed, half surrounded by a 9ft high wall.

It is believed there was a pig sty in a wood adjoining the kitchen garden, so pigs must have been kept at one time – possibly by the previous owners. Two gardeners were generally employed to tend the grounds and grow vegetables from the walled garden for the kitchen.

There was the butler's pantry, scullery, washhouse and kitchens. Beyond a flagged kitchen yard through an arched doorway, was a cobblestone stable yard with a coach house and there was an access to the kitchen garden through a doorway and stabling for two horses. There was also a room where dry food stock for the horses was kept.

An outside classroom, housing 2B in my time, was on the north side of the stable yard and above the stables in the cobbled yard was a loft where woodwork lessons were held.

There was a large garage, two more stables, a saddle room and at the end of the main entrance drive, a lodge which was occupied by Martha Moston, the cook and her husband, Joe, right up to the time the college closed and, indeed, for some while after.

When the school opened it had about 15 students, including three or four girls. In the early 1930s the numbers varied from 35 to 40 and in later years the number grew to between 80 and 100, declining again in its final years. It is not clear when the school stopped taking girls but I believe there were only four in total.

In the 1930s the school uniform consisted of a royal blue blazer with two side pockets and a breast pocket bearing the school badge and motto. During the war years there was no blazer as all suitable materials were needed for service uniforms.

But after the war, the blazer was reintroduced with a much improved design with gold braid around the neck and lapels and a braid band around the sleeves.

THE NO HOPER

As you might expect, in the 70-odd years that Woodside was a stately home, the previous owners created magnificent grounds, some of which have already been described.

These became one huge adventure playground for the students when Percy Hope opened his school and some features became legendary for generations of boys – even more famous than the cricket field, the football field and certainly the tennis court and bowling green which were seldom used in my day. In fact, I have no recollection of a bowling green at all.

There was "The Lone Pine" – a single tree in the lower half of the lawn – and, of course, the Cedar Drive – a magnificent avenue of cedar trees leading from the house to the cricket field.

Then there was the "Bottom Path" which was actually outside the school grounds and officially out-of-bounds, although for boarders it was frequently a place to rendezvous with local girls. How they managed to get romantic there I can't imagine because it was usually full of dog shit.

The path led to a small bridge under Manor Park Road from which a footpath led across the fields to Booth's Lake. Incredibly, the Bottom Path is still there although it is now largely overgrown with trees and the bridge has been bricked up.

Then there was the "Narrow Wood" between the cricket and football fields which contained a number trees suitable for tree climbing competitions – seeing who could climb to the very top and then slither down again in the quickest time. It would have given today's Health and Safety jobsworths nightmares but I don't remember anyone getting seriously hurt.

After the school closed and on Jimmy's death, Woodside and its grounds were left to his brother John who in turn sold it to James Bancroft, who lived nearby and had been a big friend of the Hope family. He sold it to a developer on condition that the kitchen garden wall remain standing.

The rumour is that Mr Bancroft did not want to be able to see the new houses being built on the college grounds from his own house. Whether this true or not, I don't know but the wall still stands – the last remaining built part of the college. It is in good condition, having been well maintained by the look of it.

Attached to the wall is a memorial plaque, paid for and erected by the Old Boys' Association. This incorrectly states that the school was founded in 1929 – the error arising from the fact that subsequent research by the association has revealed that Percy actually moved his school there two years earlier.

Nearby residents tell me they occasionally see men "of a certain age" arriving to stare at the plaque with a nostalgic look on their faces.

I have said the wall is the last remaining "built" part of the school, and it is. But the bottom half of the old football field, which towards the end of the college's life was used as a cricket field, is still there and, appropriately, is still used as a school playing field. It is now part of the playing fields of St Vincent de Paul Catholic Primary School.

When I last visited the area, a game of cricket was in progress. The children were using the brightly coloured plastic bats and balls which these days are used to introduce youngsters to cricket without the risk of picking up a few bruises in the process. In my day at Knutsford College, or even at Yorston Lodge before that, we played with the traditional, red, hard leather cricket ball, of which I am sure we all have painful memories.

No matter, I was pleased to see that one small area still being used as a school playing field. In fact, come to think about it, I think the whole of the St Vincent de Paul school is built within what was originally part of the college grounds.

THE PROSCPECTUS

Around the time Percy opened his school in Knutsford, that is, 1927, he produced a prospectus clearly designed to entice parents to send their male offspring to this new school for the sons of gentlemen. I say "around the time" because no-one seems to be able to place some of the photographs, so they may have been taken at one of Percy's previous schools.

At any rate, by the standards of the day, the prospectus was a pretty lavish publication and it must have worked because the number of students seems to have risen dramatically in a comparatively short time.

Its claims may have been justified in those early days, but they would have raised a few eyebrows among those who were there in my time.

The school was originally called "Knutsford Preparatory College" and boys were prepared for the public schools and for the Royal Navy, it stated. The principal was said to be E.P. Hope, late senior master at Bickerton House, Birkdale, senior master Kilgrimol College, St Annes-on-Sea and senior master at Chetham's College, Manchester.

Objects of the school were said to be to give more careful attention to the individual requirements of each pupil than was usual in most schools.

"The high percentage of examination successes gained under the principal from 1915 to 1927, and the continued success of all boys in every walk of life is the best proof that this object is being fulfilled," the prospectus stated.

The principal and matron (Mrs Hope) were said to take a personal interest in each boy and "a very warm relationship should exist between masters and boys, as it has been proved beyond doubt that good results are only obtainable when a boy is happy amidst his surroundings.

"They have had a life long experience of boys and believe in a jolly, happy, healthy, free, manly and brotherly way of dealing with them."

I'm not too sure how many boys felt jolly or happy, or had "brotherly" feelings towards Percy when he was wielding the cane, but there you are.

Great attention was given to secure absolutely healthy conditions of life, and no ailment or lassitude, however small, was too slight to be attended to, the prospectus continued.

The fact that the school stood on high ground, with an unbroken and extensive outlook, was said to make it more pleasant in every way.

There was "an excellent supply of town's water". The sanitary arrangements were of the most modern type and a new and lavishly furnished bathroom for the boys had just been installed at great expense.

The lavatories were said to be well constructed and disinfected daily. This might well have been the case in 1927, but the only memory I have is of a indoor toilet worryingly close to the kitchen and an external urinal, worryingly close to the dining room, which usually stank to high heaven.

The school was said to have neither cubicles nor dormitories but to simply have bedrooms which would never be allowed to become crowded and were well ventilated.

Well, crowded or not, they were always known as dormitories by everyone I ever spoke to.

Food would be of the best quality, varied, unlimited, with a substantial breakfast, lunch, inner in the middle of the day, tea with

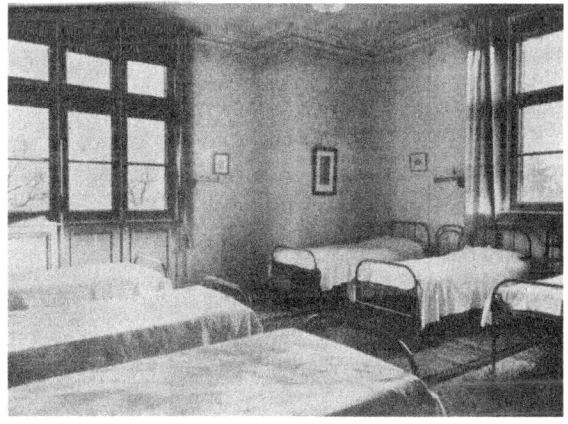

Bedroom or dormitory?

jam or cake and a light supper. As a day boy I can only speak about lunch, but if I ever took an apple to school I was invariably approached by a hungry boarder who would ask if he could have the core, so I have doubts about food being "unlimited".

Fees were 70 guineas a year in the Junior House – that's around £4,450 in 2020 prices - and 80 guineas per year in the senior house. Day boys were charged seven guineas per term – more than £500 in 2020 prices.

Various extras were charged for additional subjects such as science, German or Greek, singing, piano, typewriting, shorthand, book-keeping, dancing and riding.

A charge of seven shillings and sixpence was made per term to cover the cost of cricket and football materials and the services of a gymnastic instructor. Certainly some equipment was provided but I do not recall this including the cricket "box" or abdominal protector – and I have painful memories to bear this out.

A reading room and library was said to exist in a beautifully furnished room. Each term, a reading club would be formed, and any boy could become a member by presenting a book or paying two pence a week. Daily, weekly and monthly papers would be provide but by the time I arrived, the only papers and magazines I ever saw were the type that had to be concealed from the teaching staff.

Discipline would be firm but just, with the main purpose of the uplifting of character so that the boys could live their lives in the fulfilment of duty, rather than as a means of gaining worldly advancement alone.

Oxford and Cambridge Local Examinations would be taken in the ordinary school course and special attention would given to the sons of commercial gentlemen who desired their sons to take up commerce.

Dealing with the curriculum, the prospectus stated that mathematics would play a very important part in the school and the services of a fully qualified mathematical master would be "dovoted" (not my spelling!) entirely to this department.

We hear a lot about school uniforms these days. In 1927, Knutsford Preparatory College indicated that school caps, blazers and jerseys could be obtained at the school.

"Eton Suits are optional, but a best suit with Eton collar must be worn on Sundays and for special occasions.
"Parents are advised to let the boys wear short knickerbockers with the knees bare on weekdays. This is simply advised and not absolutely essential."
No-one I knew could remember Eton Suits or collars being worn, although some were apparently evident on early school pictures.

THE NO HOPER

PERCY AND CO

Left to right: In 1949: Mr Dawson, Jimmy Hope, Valerie Hope, Percy Hope, Mrs Booker (Matron), Denis Leighton and Freddie Forshaw

It's time I said something about the teaching staff at Knutsford College during my time there for, collectively and individually, I am sure they played a big part in shaping the characters of the students.

I must start with Percy, otherwise known as "EP" and sometimes referred to as "The Beak".

He was a colourful, bombastic character who could strike fear into the heart of any erring student with no more than a glare. He was able to instil even more fear when wielding a cane - or a riding crop.

But while he was a strict disciplinarian he could, also, display considerable kindness when the occasion demanded and undoubtedly cared deeply for those in his care.

Edward Percy Hope was born at Chorlton-cum-Hardy, Manchester, on March 17 1881, the youngest of seven children. He began his teaching career when only 18 as an assistant master at the Boys and Girls Refuge at Strangeways, Manchester - just about as far removed from a "school for the sons of gentlemen" as you could get.

THE NO HOPER

Later he was a senior master at Chetham's in Manchester - now a renowned music school but originally a charity for musically gifted children from poor backgrounds.

Percy was a talented organist and during this period sometimes played at Manchester Cathedral.

He served in the First World War as a lieutenant in the Household Cavalry but all I can say about this time of his life is that if there were many more like Percy in the British Army, it's no wonder we won the bloody war.

During this period he developed a life-long love of horses. There were always horses at the school – sometimes as many as four.

After the war he opened his first school in an old Victorian house at Bunbury, Cheshire, which he called "Heathcroft College."

His second school was at Beeston in the 1920s - it's now "The Wild Boar" a popular, upmarket restaurant – but for some time after Percy opened Knutsford College, at Woodside, in 1927, it was a girls school. The last time I was in the restaurant there were pictures of the girls school on the wall, but nothing to indicate it had ever been a boys school.

Percy must have been a busy man with an amazing capacity because around this time he was also a reservist in the Manchester Police Force. A photograph of him in police uniform on horseback hung in his office at Knutsford.

He was a bachelor, although Maria Maud Shuttleworth, matron at Bunbury and later at Beeston and Knutsford, clearly played a big part in his life and was known as "Mrs Hope". She was a widow with two sons, John and James, who both took the name Hope.

Percy on horseback with two unknown students

THE NO HOPER

Both her sons were on the teaching staff. James - otherwise known as "Mr Jimmy", became deputy head and, eventually headmaster after Percy's death. John had moved on before my time and, I believe, opened his own school in the London area.

For quite some years, initially at Beeston, then at first at Knutsford College, the Hope family were the only teachers, as the pupil numbers were only around 15 to 40. EP mainly taught scripture but first thing Monday morning he would turn up to give a quick dose of mental arithmetic. Anyone who gave the wrong answer was invariably castigated as "a Barmy Arab." By the time I arrived, he seldom took classes at all but was always present at assembly. There were still plenty of "Barmy Arabs" about, however.

Percy's talent as an organist meant he was in great demand at local churches and he frequently played at the parish churches of Knutsford, Toft, Rostherne and Hale.

One of his great loves was amateur theatre and he was a founder member of Knutsford Amateur Operatic Society, which still exists as the Knutsford Musical Theatre Company.

But I don't think his association with the society lasted long as my parents became involved with it in its early years and I am pretty sure Percy was no longer there. I recall there was a dispute between members who wanted to concentrate on Gilbert and Sullivan and others who wanted to introduce more modern shows. This led to the establishment of a rival group known as the Cranford Musical Society and I think Percy went with this group.

The college frequently put on productions itself and Percy staged his own versions of "The Mikado" and "The Gondoliers" at the Marcliff Cinema in Knutsford on several occasions. He also produced plays at the college from time to time and parents were encouraged to attend.

He formed a choir from the termly boarders. Eighteen students, two bass men singers and four ladies sang at morning service and evensong at St Mary's Church, Rostherne where Percy played the organ for some years.

THE NO HOPER

The church had no electricity, the aisles were lined with oil lamps and the organ had large bellows which had to be manually pumped - usually by one of the Knutsford College boys. The organ pump had a large handle which had to be pushed up and down to keep the bellows full. It was necessary to pump harder for bass notes than for treble.

If you over-pumped, the superfluous cold air exited at the pedals and up Percy's trouser leg - which did not best please him.

If you didn't pump hard enough the organ would issue sounds described by one boy as "like a dying cow" to the great rage of Percy and great delight of the boys.

One boy claims that on one occasion when he didn't pump hard enough, Percy bellowed: "Blow you bugger, blow"!

The boys who served in the choir were paid a small amount by the vicar each term - two half-crowns. But they also sang for occasional weddings and funerals and were paid extra for this.

The choir boys were taken to the church in an Austin 10 and an Armstrong Siddeley - the latter usually driven by Jimmy who on occasions had difficulty changing gear.

He would stamp on the clutch numerous times, uttering indecipherable oaths, until the change took place.

It was a big car and usually took about eight boys in the back and a few more in the front. As many as 13 were on occasions squeezed into the back!

There were two holes in the back of the Armstrong Siddeley, which were reputed to be bullet holes. The story was that Percy refused to stop for a Home Guard patrol during the War and that the patrol opened fire, but whether this actually happened must be considered doubtful.

The death of Maria Maud brought an end to the choir singing at Rostherne. Percy wanted her to be interred in the churchyard but the vicar said they were running out of burial space and that only local people could be buried there. Percy was outraged - and the choir joined the rest of the school for morning service at Knutsford Parish Church from then on.

THE NO HOPER

It may have been during this period that I and a number of other day boys attended confirmation classes which must have been arranged by Percy.

I remember attending the weekly classes along with Charlie Pemberton, Geoff Aldridge, Bob Jackson and a few others.

Charlie lived at Timperley and occasionally came to our house for tea before the evening classes. Often, when there was a suitable film on, we would attend the Marcliff Cinema afterwards.

Later Percy moved his pupils to the Church of St Cross which was only a few hundred yards from the school. One can only wonder why the school had not always attended this church, it was so convenient.

Percy mowing the lawn

I imagine the various vicars were quite pleased to welcome the contingent from Knutsford College to their services as it would swell the size of the congregation considerably.

The choir members were certainly disappointed when they were finally disbanded as they enjoyed the singing - and also the annual choir trip to Blackpool!

Doug Griffiths recalls one incident which illustrates the compassionate side of Percy's nature.

One Saturday morning, Doug was taking part in a "commando raid" with other boarders when he cut his lip quite badly on some barbed wire in the woods.

He was treated by Maria Maud who decided he was not fit to go on the weekly visit to the Marcliff Cinema.

She handed him over to Percy who took him to his office, sat him down in his chair and gave him something to eat and drink. He then entertained him all afternoon with tales of his life.

"I wish I could remember all that he told me," said Doug, years later. "I soon forgot about missing the film show and realised that he wasn't quite

THE NO HOPER

the ogre I had always believed him to be. After that day he always appeared to me in a different light."

Percy wasn't without a sense of humour – particularly after a few pints. When he wasn't at the Legh Arms, the nearest pub to the college, he could often be found among a group of regulars at either the White Lion or the Angel in King Street.

Another member of the group was one Ernest E. Wakefield, better known as "Wakey", editor for many years of the Knutsford Guardian, whose offices were right opposite the two pubs.

Wakey was a bluff Yorkshireman and a great character who could give and take a joke and the other members of the group, Percy included, loved to play tricks on him in the hope of getting them into print.

The Angel at this time was famous for having a parrot in a cage in the bar and Percy and Co. put a hen's egg in the cage. When Wakey arrived for a swift pint they told him the parrot had laid an egg.

Incredibly for a seasoned journalist, Wakey fell for it and a story subsequently appeared in the Guardian about the parrot that had laid an egg.

Percy and his friends thought it a huge joke – particularly as it was a male parrot. But Wakey had the last laugh. He sold the story on to several national newspapers and earned a considerable sum of money.

Another trick the group played on Wakey was even more incredible – so much so that I wouldn't have believed it if I hadn't seen it myself in the Guardian files when I started work there, years later. I can still hardly believe Wakey fell for it because the same trick had been played on a number of other newspapers previously.

Percy played a leading role in this jape. He told Wakey an ancient Roman urn had been unearthed in the college grounds. It bore the inscription "Thi sisapi spo tan dati none" which he was attempting to get translated from the Latin.

Wakey duly published a story about it – apparently not realising that if the letters were spaced differently they read "This is a pis pot and a tin one."

THE NO HOPER

Percy died, aged 72, on Friday, August 24, 1951 of heart disease and rheumatism. He had suffered a serious illness some time before that but had apparently recovered and still seemed fit and well, regularly appearing at an upstairs window and bellowing at any pupil he saw misbehaving in the grounds. I do not know if this illness played any part in his death, later, for he did return to duty after a while and appeared to be his old, irascible self.

According to his funeral report in the Knutsford Guardian he had been in failing health during that last term, and only managed to keep going because of his strength of character and devotion to the boys in his care. But to me, he still seemed indestructible. I saw no clue, not even a hint, when the school broke up for the summer holiday, that he would not still be there, brandishing his cane, when we returned.

There was a big funeral at Knutsford Parish Church, attended by many local dignitaries, teachers, old boys, pupils and parents.

Former pupil Richard Aldridge, the talented musician who had in earlier years played the piano for hymns at morning assembly, played the organ. The pall-bearers were six old boys from the 1930-1935 period - Roy Sheppard, Norman Wood, Wilf Stanier, John Clarkson, Bill Steele, and Horace Townsend.

According to Wilf Stanier a group of old boys used to meet regularly at The White Lion and, over the years, Percy would occasionally drop in and buy them a pint. He allegedly said, on more than one occasion: "I may not have taught you buggers much, but at least I taught you how to drink."

A couple of days after Percy's death, Jimmy walked in on the group and said: "You, You, You and You, detailed pall-bearers for Mr Hope's funeral Monday next week".

They were all proud to oblige.

During the funeral service, the vicar, the Rev R.A.M. Harris, described Percy as "Knutsford's Mr Chips" – a description I think Percy would have approved of.

THE NO HOPER

Percy, Maria Maude and Jimmy are all buried in a family grave at Knutsford Cemetery in Tabley Road. All three bear the name Hope.

Mr Jimmy

Jimmy Hope was too fond of the drink. His life was a tragic story of a fine man with a brilliant academic mind being destroyed by alcohol. He had lived too long in the shadow of the formidable Percy and this, combined with the effects of drink, probably hastened the closure of the college. It certainly shortened his life.

In earlier years, during his time as deputy head and even as head, he managed to keep a degree of control over his drinking. Certainly the younger boys were unaware of the situation.

But the older boys and, I am sure, other members of the staff knew all about it. He taught First Class for maths last period before lunch, probably in the mistaken belief

he could leave the senior boys working diligently while he slipped off to the nearby Legh Arms for liquid refreshment.

In fact, the class descended into anarchy within minutes of his departure.

But I can't stress too much, Jimmy was a well educated and extremely intelligent man and, if you got him on the right day, a good teacher.

He was born in 1904 at Great Lever in Bolton and was the third of four children born to Herbert and Maria Maude Shuttleworth - who we have already met as a result of her relationship with Percy. So he was, in effect, Percy's stepson, although I, for one, never knew that. If I thought anything at all, I thought he was Percy's son.

He was known throughout his teaching career as "Mr Jimmy". Little is known of his early life, but it is believed he went to Chetham's for teacher training.

He became a teacher in his early twenties at Percy's first school at Bunbury, where he taught Maths and Literature and, later, at Knutsford. But he was well able to fill-in on other subjects when required to do so and

THE NO HOPER

it was relatively easy to persuade him talk about almost any subject if you were not looking forward to maths that day.

"Sir, is it correct to clean your teeth up and down or from side to side?"

"Sir, did King Canute really come to Knutsford?"

Jimmy was known to have strong views about this. He was dismissive of the theory that Canute had visited Knutsford and forded the River Lily and that as a result the town became known as Cunetesford and, eventually, Knutsford.

He claimed to have seen an old map which referred to "Knott's Ford" which he believed was a much more likely origin of the name.

If he is ever proved correct, it will come as a bit of a shock to Knutsford Town Council who some years ago arranged for a statue of Canute to be erected in the grounds of the council offices!

Still, one of Jimmy's favourite sayings was: "A man who never made a mistake never made anything" so I don't think we should be arranging for the statue to be removed just yet.

For a while when I was in First Class he taught Scripture – and showed he had a good knowledge of the Bible. We were reading Genesis one day when Jimmy suddenly announced that not much was happening for the next few chapters so we would skip forward a bit.

Innocent that I was, I took him at his word, but some of my classmates were more suspicious and took the trouble to read the pages we had skipped. They discovered a passage which described how Onan slept with his brother's widow but "spilled his seed on the ground" so as not to give his brother an heir.

Our teacher clearly thought we were not ready for such revelations – even when they were in the Bible!

Jimmy had strong views on many issues. Woe betide the boy he caught breathing through his mouth.

"Close your mouth boy – do you want to look like a simpleton?"

Woe betide anyone who used the letter "O" instead of the figure "0". I heard him berate telephone operators about this on numerous occasions –

THE NO HOPER

there was a telephone in the hall, just outside the room occupied by First Class when I was in it and we could all hear him. I felt genuinely sorry for the "Hello Girls" when I heard him ranting on at them.

Jimmy was also an accomplished woodworker - his father had been a carpenter - and taught carpentry to those boys whose parents were prepared to pay an extra 10 shillings. I went home and told my Dad about this and he gave me a 10 bob note to take to school. But when the time came I did not know where the woodwork class was held, was too timid to ask anyone, so just didn't go I pocketed the money and, to convince my parents I was actually attending the carpentry classes, cadged items made by other boys - usually model boats - which I took home with great displays of pride. I don't recall that any of them were great masterpieces but they seemed to impress my parents, who clearly stll did not have great expectations of me. What I did with the 10 shillings I don't know.

Jimmy was particularly adept at building caravans and spent many hours in the evenings and weekends building caravans that he later sold, usually at least one per year. At times there were numerous caravans dotted around the school grounds.

He remained a bachelor until the age of 40, when he married Valerie Joan Moore, nee Bond, at Rostherne Church on August 1, 1945. Valerie was a widow whose husband had died some years previously. She had three sons, Michael, Rory and Martin who all subsequently attended Knutsford College and seemed to treat Jimmy as their father.

After Percy died, Jimmy made strenuous efforts to keep Knutsford College going as a viable concern.

The general opinion among students was that he did not have Percy's business experience. He could still control a class – when he wasn't at the Legh Arms - and he was well able to impart some knowledge to those boys prepared to learn.

But he seemed to have difficulty recruiting capable teachers and most new members of staff did not stay long.

It is believed that after the college closed in 1954 he taught for a while at Pownall Hall School, Wilmslow - one of the independent schools we occasionally played at football or cricket.

The college was converted - in a fashion - into flats and Jimmy and Valerie moved into one of them, living on the proceeds of letting the others and caravans dotted around the grounds.

In 1957 they separated, leaving a devastated Jimmy to live alone in a rapidly deteriorating building. He tried to persuade Valerie to return to him but she would not and eventually married for a third time.

Jimmy died, aged 55, on February 29, 1960.

Denis

Ask any former student who attends the annual Old Boys Reunion, who his favourite teacher was and the answer will invariably be "Denis."

I firmly believe that if I learned anything much at Knutsford College, it was mainly thanks to Denis Leighton. He was an ever-present member of the teaching staff during all but my final year at the college – which was also the school's final year. In fact, although it is widely believed the school finally closed because Jimmy lacked the business acumen that Percy had possessed, I think it had just as much to do with Denis leaving.

Born in Ireland in 1919, he had a wonderful Irish accent. An educated Irish accent, that is.

I didn't know it at the time, but he apparently lived in a small room between the junior and senior dormitories, which was a little inconvenient for the boys who slept in those rooms as they had to be much quieter than those who slept in another dormitory further away down a passage.

He was a formidable swimmer, specialising in the Australian crawl and used to take a party of boys to Northwich Swimming Baths early on a Wednesday morning.

THE NO HOPER

Every Sunday afternoon, after the compulsory writing of the weekly letter home, Denis would take a party of boarders for a walk, down various lanes, and through the woods, during which time he would chat to the boys all the way there and all the way back. He had an amazing knowledge of almost every subject under the sun and an even more amazing ability to pass that knowledge on. More than one boy has remarked that they learned more on those walks than they did in the classroom.

As a day boy, I missed out on these walks and talks, but in the classroom and on occasions during lunch or break periods when Denis was perfectly willing to go on "teaching" I soon learned that he was a fount of all knowledge.

We occasionally had "free" periods in class when we could ask for our favourite subjects to be taught. I was particularly interested in astronomy and prehistory. Denis was an expert on both subjects and could easily be persuaded to talk at length on either subject. These days, thanks to TV and films, every youngster seems to know all there is to know about dinosaurs but I am pretty sure that I wouldn't even have heard of them but for Denis.

I also recall him displaying considerable knowledge of jazz, and in particular the pianist "Jelly Roll" Morton – who most of us had never heard of. He was able to discuss the subtleties of Mr Morton's music but also complete his lecture by expressing the view that his nickname was probably more to do with his sexual prowess than his music.

He knew how to maintain discipline without using force. While I know other Old Boys have spoken of him using a metal ruler on the knuckles to keep order, I have no memory of this.

In fact, looking back on it, I think I might have been one of Denis's favourites, although he probably made us all feel like that. He certainly encouraged me to write during a period when he was teaching English, as well as Maths, History and Geography.

We were regularly set an essay to write and Denis would read out the one he considered to be the best. Invariably it was mine.

THE NO HOPER

One week, we were told we could write an essay on any subject we chose. I got half way through mine and then, suddenly, thought of a subject which inspired me rather more. I scrapped the original and started the new one – which was completely different.

The boy sitting next to me looked amazed and said: "Don't you want that?"

"No," said I. "You can have it if you want."

My friend took over my original essay, rewriting it in his own hand and continuing on from where I left off.

When Denis came to read out the best essay he, as usual, chose mine. But when he had finished he said that, unusually, the other boy had produced a good piece of work. He read it out to the class until he reached the very word where I had left off.

"After that, it wasn't much good," he said.

I remember another occasion when Denis was taking us for cricket – well, I would, wouldn't I?

For some reason, we were not using the cricket field but the bottom half of the football field which was usually not used for anything. It was not really big enough for cricket and Denis, no doubt fearing a flurry of lost balls, announced at the start of the match that "sixes" would not be allowed.

I was captain of one team and decided to try and bat through most of the team's innings, blocking studiously to make sure I was not out. When the last ball arrived, we needed six to win – and I whacked it clean over the hedge to land first-bounce in the middle of Manor Park Road.

"Six!" bellowed Denis.

There was an immediate uproar from the other team.

"Sir - you said sixes were not allowed!"

"Six!" bellowed Denis again. And that was that!

Denis left Knutsford College about a year before it closed. It was rumoured he had left because he had not been paid.

"He was wearing sandals during the thick snow because he could not afford a proper pair of shoes," I was told.

THE NO HOPER

I don't know how true that was, but Denis was soon employed at the Ilford film company's Rajar Works, at Mobberley. According to Joe Ashley he had become a "scientist." Again, I don't know how true that was, but it certainly wouldn't have surprised me.

One day in November, 1972, by which time I was married, living in the Warrington area and had an eight year-old son, my wife and I went to visit my parents in Knutsford. My Mum silently handed me a folded copy of that week's Knutsford Guardian which contained a report of a road accident in Hollow Lane – about a quarter of-a-mile from where the college had been and part of my daily walk to school.

Tragically, two people had been killed. One was a local man named Peter Allen, who I had known well in my youth. The other was Denis Leighton, aged 53.

I cried my eyes out.

Freddie

Captain Frederick Forshaw was, or appeared to be, a fixture at the college during most of my time there.

Known to most of us as "Freddie" behind his back, he was "Captain Forshaw" to his face.

I have memories that often, when he was addressed as "Captain" he would respond cheerfully by saying: "Who knows me in Kathmandu?", or Istanbul, or some other far flung place, which gave the impression that he had served in the Army is various parts of the world. Whether he had, in fact, is another matter. But he certainly was an ex-Army man and he certainly had achieved the rank of captain.

Freddie was born in Lancashire in 1897 and lived with his parents, Joseph and Louise Forshaw at Ormskirk where he gained employment as a clerk. He met and later married Florence Irene Maddox, from Newsham Park in 1919, but the marriage ended in a divorce a few years later.

THE NO HOPER

He then spent some years in the Army but on returning to civvy street he worked as a cotton salesman and later became a member of the Hope "family" by virtue of marrying Valerie Bond's sister, Dorothea, who was then working at the Royal George Hotel in Knutsford. They were married in 1929.

During my time at the college, Freddie lived at the Dun Cow pub at Ollerton. I am guessing that Dorothea's experience at the Royal George enabled her to acquire the licence for the Dun Cow, because I am pretty sure it was not held by Freddie. The Royal George is now just a memory, but in those days it was the most prestigious hotel in the Knutsford area, frequently playing host to celebrities. I recall that during my time as a reporter on the Knutsford Guardian I interviewed the film actor Tyrone Power there - and he was only one of many famous people who visited.

Freddie helped out with teaching at Knutsford College – mainly as the sports master.

I got on well with him, mainly because he seemed to favour cricket over football. Well, I would, wouldn't I?

One memory I have of him followed an incident when I was disciplined, rather unfairly I thought, by Jimmy. It was during the mid-day free period which, for day boys, took place while the boarders were having lunch. There was a group of us in a class room because it was raining. Myself and a couple of other boys were on one side of the room, studying quietly and another group were on the other side behaving badly and creating a din.

Suddenly Jimmy burst into the room and demanded to know who was responsible for the noise. Of course, no-one owned up so he then proceeded to give us all a dressing down, apparently thinking we were all creating the uproar which he had presumably heard from some other part of the building. He handed out some minor punishment – I can't remember what – and then stormed out.

There was a few moments silence and then I turned indignantly to the culprits and said: "Hey – why didn't you lot own up – we weren't making any noise!"

THE NO HOPER

Unfortunately for me, Jimmy was still outside and heard me.

He burst back in and roared: "Who was that?"

I had little choice but to stand and meekly say: "It was me, Sir."

"Come out here boy," he bellowed and when I reached the front of the classroom he grabbed me by my lapels and proceeded to shake me violently. At least that was his intention.

I was a big lad. Probably getting around six foot tall by that time and pretty hefty too.

One of the onlookers told me later that during that shaking, I remained pretty motionless while Jimmy, who was not of a particularly robust stature, was himself shaking back and to.

But the shaking was not the end of my punishment. Perhaps because he realised his actions had somewhat backfired on him, Jimmy then proceeded to administer what he undoubtedly knew would really hurt me most

He banned me from games that week.

In the winter that would not have bothered me but this was summer and that meant missing cricket!

That was an end to it as far as he was concerned and I spent the next couple of days thinking I would not be playing cricket that week. Well, I would, wouldn't I?

But on games day, in the morning, Freddie stopped me in a corridor near the cloakroom.

"Skentelbery," he said, "I don't know that you have been banned from games." And walked away before I could say anything. Needless to say, I played.

Freddie was also an accomplished artist and occasionally taught art.

After the college closed, he and his wife moved to Earls Croome near Upton on Severn, Worcester, and ran a general store and café until his death in 1963 at the age of 66. Dorothea remained at Earls Croom until her death in 1980 aged 80.

THE NO HOPER

William Fairburn

I lived in fear of Mr Fairburn. And I mean fear.

He taught maths for most of the time I was in 2B and I was a complete duffer when it came to maths and neither Mr Fairburn nor anyone else who has ever attempted to teach me has ever managed to explain its mysteries. Simple addition, subtraction, division and multiplication weren't too bad. At least I could see they had a purpose. But after that, it just seemed to me to be pointless.

Mr Fairburn had a habit of setting some work on the blackboard and expecting his pupils to then get on with it.

As an example of how hopeless I was, he would set out examples of something he referred to as "long division" on the blackboard and then expect us to produce similar work in our exercise books.

He would then start to pace around the classroom, passing behind each row of desks. Occasionally he would stop behind a pupil and give the impression of studying his work over his shoulder.

He probably wasn't – or perhaps he had very bad eyesight and could not see well enough to see what the wretched boy in front of him was writing.

I have come to this conclusion because I had no idea at all how to do "long division" and would simply write figures down, roughly in the shape of the examples he had written on the blackboard.

You know the old saying that if you put a million monkeys down at a million typewriters they would eventually come up with the complete works of Shakespeare? Well, those were the sort of odds against me ever getting the correct answer to one of Mr Fairburn's sums. I just wrote anything down and the result would be complete gibberish.

Yet Mr Fairburn would frequently stop behind me and I would sit there, convinced that he was looking at my work and expecting at any moment to be dealt a hefty blow across the back of the head. But it never happened and Mr Fairburn would eventually move on to terrorise some other boy without ever making comment on my work.

THE NO HOPER

It is only in later years that I have realised that Mr Fairburn didn't give a damn for my work and that I probably had nothing to fear from him.

At the time I was literally terrified of him, so much so that he drove me to the verge of a nervous breakdown.

I think it would be recognised as such nowadays but in those days my behaviour would only be seen as "swinging the lead."

What started to happen was that shortly after I arrived at school, I would develop a headache, which came on gradually until it reached a level where it just wiped me out. It would start during drill and would have reached an unbearable level by the time the first lesson started. I was completely unable to take any further part in any lesson.

Some time during the lunch period it would begin to wear off and by afternoon it would have completely gone.

This didn't just happen occasionally – it happened every day and of course it was not long before Percy found out about it. I remember one day noticing him standing on the terrace after lunch, looking at me as I played happily with some other boys.

A short time later, as we filed back into school I walked passed Percy in the hall.

He glared at me, said something that sounded like "headaches my arse!" and gave me a clip across the head.

Soon after that, word of this strange phenomenon afflicting their son reached my parents, presumably via Percy. I was taken to the doctor's and examined and from there sent to an optician because it had been decided the headaches were caused by poor eyesight.

The optician did, indeed, find my sight was not as it should be and that I needed spectacles. But first I would have to have a course of eye drops which, he predicted, would make my vision blurred for several weeks. As I would be unable to read, he advised that I should be kept off school.

So I started an unexpected "holiday" which seemed to last for about a month, during which time I could not read because my vision was completely blurred. I could read large newspaper headlines, or the wording of billboards in the street, but normal print was incomprehensible.

When the blurring stopped and I was able to see properly again, I was given an eyesight test and prescribed spectacles. The headaches had ceased as soon as I stopped going to school so I was able to return, complete with my new glasses which I was to wear for reading and close work only. The headaches did not return – even though, after, a couple of months, I lost my spectacles and never had them replaced.

I don't recall Mr Fairburn and his terrifying maths lessons being an issue any more. I did not wear spectacles again until in my teens and after starting work so I strongly suspect that, if the same thing were to happen these days, I would have been referred to a child psychiatrist rather than an optician!

I think the headaches would have been diagnosed as migraines, brought on by stress. I have never had them since, but I know how bad they can be as my mother, my mother-in-law and my wife have all suffered from them.

Ivor Morris

I liked Mr Morris, who taught English Literature, which was one of my favourite subjects. My recollection is that most lessons consisted of him reading to us.

He had formerly been a professional, Shakespearian actor, although I did not know this at the time. My recollection is of a very laid-back man with a casual approach to teaching.

He fell from favour with Percy and Jimmy when they discovered he had selected "The Blue Lagoon" to read to 2B.

At the time, a film based on this book had caused quite a stir in the press because of its subject matter.

It told the story of two children, brother and sister, who were shipwrecked on a desert island with one other survivor – an aging seaman.

THE NO HOPER

They were marooned for years, during which time the two children grew up with no education other than what the old seaman could give them.
He did his best – but neglected to tell them about the birds and the bees or that brothers and sisters could not form relationships. He eventually died and the two youngsters grew up, eventually falling in love and having a baby.
Later they were rescued and the horror of what had happened became known.
The film of the book starred Donald Houston and Jean Simmons – who became probably the first woman to draw to my attention the fact that the opposite sex was, well, rather different! I'm not sure how I came to notice her as I certainly wasn't allowed to see the film.
Like many teachers, Mr Morris took great delight in ridiculing students for "schoolboy howlers." When, during a geography lesson, he asked John Cotterill what fish were caught at the Dogger Bank, John's reply, after great thought, was: "Kippers" – which reduced the class to hysterics. But, given that a kipper is generally a smoked herring, was John all that wrong? On another occasion Mr Morris asked one hapless boy: "What do you clean your top teeth with?"
The boy replied:"A toothbrush, sir."
"And your bottom?"
"A toothbrush, sir."
Mr Morris: "I use paper." Again the class was in hysterics.

Mr Dawson

Many other teachers came and went during my time at Knutsford College One who stands out in my memory was Mr Dawson. He was a strict disciplinarian who demanded high standards from pupils – and as far as I know, no student ever got to know his first name.

THE NO HOPER

On his first day he was taking, I think, 2A, when Neville Kaye, a close friend of mine, who was sitting on the back row, let out a long and loud belch.

Neville had developed belching to a fine art. He could speak in belches and instigated a series of belching and farting contests, which always attracted a great deal of interest.

The idea was to say a lengthy word or phrase in one belch. Words such as "Archbishop" or "Archipelago" were popular choices. Neville usually won and I remember one of his classics was "Baa-baa black sheep have you any wool?" Another was "Archbishops and Little Fishes."

On this day, however, he simply let rip with a long, loud, rich belch that today would have attracted admiration in the sound effects department of "Jurassic Park" or some other film about dinosaurs. It did not go down well with Mr Dawson however.

He leapt to his feet and barked: "Who was that?"

Neville, who was more accustomed to receiving praise for his belching, was shocked. So much so that he rose to his feet and said: "Me sir."

"Excuse yourself immediately," said Mr Dawson.

"Excuse me, sir. I apologise," said Neville.

Nothing more was said, but everyone in the class knew from that day that Mr Dawson would not tolerate belching or any other coarse behaviour in the classroom.

Soon after, presumably after he had settled in at the school, he began to administer summary justice of a particularly painful kind - rapping you on the knuckles with the edge of a ruler. Hard.

I received this punishment on several occasions, usually for the most trivial of misdemeanours.

One thing I particularly remember was being punished for yawning.

"Skentelbery," he roared, on seeing my gaping mouth. "Are you tired or bored?"

"Tired, sir," I replied.

"Right, come out here – I'll wake you up."

THE NO HOPER

I got about six sharp raps on the knuckles and was, indeed, woken up.
Some days later, he caught me yawning again.
"Skentelbery! Are you tired or bored?"
Remembering what had happened on the previous occasion, I replied:
"Bored, sir."
"Bored, are you?" he roared.
"Come out here and I will teach you not to be bored during my class."
I suffered an even more painful session with the ruler, which left my knuckles bruised for weeks.
After that, bruised knuckles were a familiar sight after one of Mr Dawson's classes.

The others

A teacher of a completely different type was Mr Edwards, an elderly man who was a Spiritualist and occasionally gave us lessons based on works such as "Outward Bound", a play and novel dating from the early 1920s which espoused the notion that you could contact deceased people in an afterlife.
He was a fairly timid man and one day I felt emboldened during a free period to ask him if he would tell us something about his experiences in the Crimean War (1853-1856).
He didn't react in any way and later I realised it was a very insensitive attempt at humour on my part.
An even more timid teacher was Mr Southgate. He was tall, thin and moustached and possessed a somewhat shrill, squeaky voice. He didn't last very long and after his departure a rumour went round that he had fled the school, running down the drive carrying a small suitcase which contained all his possessions and which burst opened halfway down the drive, spilling the contents all over the place.

THE NO HOPER

David Wrigley was another mild-mannered man who stayed at the school for quite a long time and taught a variety of subjects.

He was very young and inexperienced and fell foul of a pupil, who I think was named Jones, who was, shall we say, difficult to control in the classroom. He would openly argue with Mr Wrigley who did his best to keep the unruly element of the class under control but, in the case of Jones, failed miserably.

Jones would frequently walk out of class and go wandering off around the grounds. The rest of us would sit in class and occasionally see him stroll passed with his hands in his pockets.

I was a reasonably well behaved pupil around this time and got on well with Mr Wrigley who, I realised was doing his best. He became quite friendly with Bob Jackson – one of my closer friends – and visited his home once when I was there and seemed to be on good terms with Bob's parents.

But one day I must have been in a bit of Bolshie mood and started to give cheek and generally refuse to co-operate with whatever Mr Wrigley was trying to do.

Eventually he lost his patience and threatened me with some minor form of disciplinary action.

"Why me?" I protested. "You let Jones walk out of the class and do whatever he likes."

"Jones is a fool!" he retorted.

I had no answer to that because I knew he was right. I had always thought Jones was daft, in effect walking out on an education which was being provided for his own benefit and which his parents were paying for.

I think I treated David Wrigley with a bit more respect after that – particularly when I learned that he had the autograph of my dream girl – Jean Simmons.

He showed it to a number of us one day and I studied it and tried to compare it to one I had at home on a photograph of the actress.

"That's not her autograph," I said. "It's nothing like the one I have got."

THE NO HOPER

"Well I saw her sign it," he replied, "So I would be a bit worried about the one you have got if I were you."
Looking back, I wonder about the maturity of a schoolmaster who collected autographs of film stars. But at the time, it only enhanced his reputation because autograph collecting was quite popular in those days. My own collection was mainly of cricketers and Miss Simmons was allowed a place in it only because, as I mentioned earlier, she was the first female to catch my eye.
I can't remember how I acquired her signature – if, indeed, it was her's – but I know I didn't see her sign it. I suspect it was as a result of sending a stamped addressed envelope to the film studio.
The Knutsford College Old Boys Association website lists 53 members of staff who served at the college during the period 1919 to 1954 but some were not teachers and some presumably were in Percy's employ at his earlier schools. Some of their names are familiar to me, but I have no recollection of actually knowing them.
As a day boy I had little contact with the domestic staff, such as Martha Moston, the cook, her husband Joe and Sam Lancaster who both seemed to be gardener handymen. But they were great characters and all students, particularly the boarders, had a high regard for them.
There was an ex-serviceman known simply as "Tucker" who was brought in by Jimmy for a while to do some maintenance work in the grounds.
I remember him chopping down the big oak tree by the cricket ground which had, in happier times, served as a score board.
At break times he would attract a crowd of students and take great pleasure in telling them how he had won the war single-handedly.
The last new teacher to arrive before the college closed was Mr Goldrick.
He came after Denis Leighton's departure and did his best to keep the school going during its final year.
Like Denis, he was Irish, and my recollection was that he was a fair man and quite a good teacher.

THE NO HOPER

One thing he did was to re-introduce rugby to the school so for a while we had football and rugby alternate weeks during the winter.
It was said he had played rugby for Birmingham University, which might or might not have been something to crow about. But certainly it impressed those of us who took any interest in the game for men with odd shaped balls!

The French Teacher

One teacher deserves special mention - Roger Aptaker, who taught French.
I was not very good at French, which is probably why I have few classroom memories of him. I knew he had served in World War 2 and was under the impression that he was one of those ex-servicemen who came out of the Army without a job and was taken on as a teacher with few if any qualifications to teach.
However, given that he taught French, I now know that he was probably well qualified. He had been a member of the Special Operations Executive, French Section, and served in the underground movement in France, working with the French Resistance and training saboteurs. As such, he would have needed to speak French well enough to deceive any Germans he might run into. And he certainly ran into a few!
I knew nothing of this at the time and I doubt if many pupils did, but Geoff Tomlinson and Johnny Steele got to know him well and on one occasion were invited to his home – a 17th century thatched cottage in Brook Street, Knutsford, which sadly no longer exists. While there, he told them a number of hair-raising tales of his wartime experiences.
Apparently he was parachuted into central France during the night wearing a lounge suit. After landing and burying his 'chute he made his way to the local railway station and bought a ticket. He stayed near the car park until

THE NO HOPER

the train arrived and then got into an empty compartment only to find it had been reserved for German soldiers.

He moved to another compartment and pretended to be asleep. When he got off the train and looked for the way out of the station he realised that he would have to pass through a German checkpoint. He put his identification card and travel pass between his teeth, his radio transmitter in one hand and a suitcase full of French francs for the Resistance in the other and slowly walked up to and through the checkpoint and out of the station - all of this in his first 24 hours in France.

His cover story was that he was a French wood cutter, cutting down trees to make charcoal which was then used to make gas to run cars and vans on. According to Roger, The Resistance discovered that if you urinated on the charcoal after it was made, it stopped it from making gas!

On another occasion, Roger and a number of Resistance fighters were racing away from the scene of a sabotage exploit, chased by German soldiers. They were in an old car with a split windscreen with a steel divider down the middle and just when they thought they had left their pursuers behind a German soldier stepped out in front of them with a sub-machine gun and sprayed the car with bullets.

Amazingly, no-one was hit and they careered on in the car, eventually leaving the enemy soldiers behind. When they got to their hideout they surveyed the damage to the car and discovered a bullet stuck in the windscreen divider. When he sat in the driver's seat, Roger realised the line of fire led straight to where his head would have been.

Years later, Geoff Tomlinson recalled: "To remember the day, Roger gave us forged million mark banknotes and German cap badges and his French wife served us glasses of lemonade and a piece of cake."

Geoff's recollection is that Knutsford College seemed to have a new French teacher every term – and I agree with him. As a result we never seemed to get passed "the pen of my aunt."

Heroics were not confined to members of staff.

THE NO HOPER

On one occasion, the exploits of two students made the national press and resulted in the pair being commended by the chairman of the bench at Knutsford Magistrates Court.

A group of boys were playing cricket when they became aware of a commotion on the nearby Manor Park Road. There was shouting and what sounded like a police whistle.
Both teams left the field and raced over to see what was going on.
They saw a man who looked like a tramp running along the road with the police about 100 yards behind him.
The boys joined the chase which turned out to be quite a long one, crossing Mobberley Road and a railway line. The older boys were gradually catching up with the man but the police had fallen far behind.
Eventually, only two boys remained in the chase - Peter Hamman and Harry Davey. The rest had been cut off by a train passing on the railway track.
During the chase, the tramp had shed several layers of clothing
The two boys grabbed the him as he attempted to climb over a fence and he fell to the ground – spilling a large amount of stolen silverware from under his remaining coat.
There was a brief struggle before the boys managed to subdue him in an arm lock and hold him until the police arrived.
It turned out the "tramp" was an RAF deserter who had broken into one of the large houses in Manor Park Road and stolen valuable property.
He had previously burgled the Royal George Hotel in Knutsford.
The man later appeared before the local magistrates and was jailed for 12 months. The chairman of the bench praised the two schoolboys and the case was reported in the Daily Mail who stated that the offender had been brought down by a "flying rugby tackle."
Whether this was due to some journalistic licence by the newspaper reporter, some exaggeration by a solicitor in court or whether there really was a "rugby tackle" we shall probably never know.
Perhaps the man was "tackled" as he climbed the fence!

THE BLAZER

As far as I have been able to find out, there is only one half-decent picture of a Knutsford College blazer in existence – and that one is on me!

I find it quite surprising that my parents went to the trouble of having a photograph taken of me in my school uniform. I was, after all, a No Hoper, in their opinion. But a leaflet came through our door one day advertising a company who would come to your home and take professional colour photos of your children which would be of studio quality. In exchange for a fee, of course.

Among the many claims the company made was that their files were open to inspection by film companies and model agencies who were always on the lookout for talent. I doubt if this claim had anything to do with persuading my Dad to part with some of his hard-earned cash, but I read the leaflet from start to finish and was immediately convinced.

I was on the road to stardom, I thought. Not as a model – even I would not have considered that a possibility. I had suffered too many cracks about being overweight at school to ever consider myself model material. But film companies – that was a different matter. They would have many different requirements and surely would see me, in my smart new blazer, as suitable for some kind of role.

THE NO HOPER

The very fact that I could have such aspirations says something about the confidence-building aspect of a Knutsford College education. The timid creature who had arrived at the school not that long before would never have had such thoughts.

However I had clearly not changed much in my parents' eyes. When I mentioned the possibility of a film career to my Mum, her swift response was: "Don't be ridiculous."

I don't remember much about the photo shoot but when the picture finally arrived it must have impressed my parents because they shelled out for a framed, coloured enlargement which I still have today and which is reproduced on the back cover of this book. In those days, colour photography was still in its infancy and the colour was, I think, added later by a separate process in the laboratory.

The rosy cheeks the process gave me made me look like something fresh from a funeral director's chapel of rest, but in other respects it wasn't at all bad and the blazer did look quite smart. It didn't stay like that for long, of course and I fancy I went through a couple of them during my time at the school. Looking at the picture today I can't see how or why I acquired the reputation of being a fat bugger. I'm prepared to accept I had some puppy fat to lose, but not that bloody much!

Wearing the blazer and accompanying blue cap out of school hours, marked one out as being from "that posh college up in Over Knutsford" so I didn't wear them much around town for fear of being set-upon by packs of less-fortunate boys from state schools. But they did make it easier to get in the cinema half-price.

I remember going to the Marcliff once with Neville Kaye, just after he had left school and was full of the joys of being an adult in full-time paid employment.

THE NO HOPER

When he saw I was wearing my school cap, he insisted I put it in my pocket as he didn't want to be seen out with a schoolboy. I agreed, but as we approached the cinema I took it out and put it on.

At the kiosk, Neville paid first and paid the full price. I asked for a half-price ticket and the cashier was about to give me one when Neville, in a loud "stage whisper" said: "Bloody big half."

"I heard that" said the cashier – and I had to put forward a lengthy argument to prove my age while a queue formed behind us in the foyer. After that, I continued to carry the cap around in my pocket to get half-price whenever possible - even after the school had closed!

THE HAUNTED MANSION

I wish Russell Blenkinsop had been a student at Knutsford College. He was a friend of mine around the time I started there and was about the same age, so if his parents had shown a similar lack of wisdom to mine they could well have sent him there too.

Not that he was shy. Far from it – he was outrageously extrovert and bossed me around something terrible. So why would I want him as a classmate?

Well, for a start, he had an unusual name which might have diverted away from me some of the ribald humour I had to put up with. Also, he was, shall I say, somewhat rotund in stature. In fact, to put it bluntly, he was a fat bugger – far fatter than I was. So again, he might have siphoned off some of the unwelcome ridicule I suffered on account of my own chubby build. And even if he did neither he was a friend who would have stuck up for me when I found myself in one of the many difficult situations that haunted my first few months.

I lost touch with him shortly after starting at Percy's academy. I think his parents moved away from Knutsford, but we were still close during my early days and I was able to tell him something of my adventures and, more likely, misadventures at my new school. One story intrigued him in particular - the legend of the haunted mansion.

Thorneyholme has already been mentioned in this chronicle – the huge, decaying property which occupied large, overgrown grounds adjacent to the college. It was bigger than Woodside although not quite as old. It had

Thorneyholme - before the US Army moved in

THE NO HOPER

been built around 1886 by wealthy businessman Charles John Galloway, who would not have wanted to live in a property smaller than his neighbour. Probably in its earlier days it would have been much grander. But it had not been as well cared for as Woodside, or other mansions in the area – certainly not after the United States entered World War 2 and it was taken over by hordes of American soldiers who effectively trashed it before going off to take part in the D Day landings.

When the lady who had owned the building before the war returned to reclaim her property she apparently walked in, looked around and walked out again never to return.

Thorneyholme then stood empty and crumbling for some years and that is how it was when I arrived at the college next door. It was, of course, "out of bounds" to students, but that did not stop many from paying the occasional visit. Malcolm Nott and John Moreton were two such and on one expedition they wandered all around the interior and then up on to the roof – probably a somewhat risky adventure considering the condition of the place.

I had not been at the college long when I heard the rumour that Thorneyholme was haunted. It may well have been a rumour started for the benefit of impressionable new boys, because I have never heard tell of it since. But Thorneyholme certainly looked spooky, even by daylight and I could only imagine what it would look like by dark. However, I did not really believe in ghosts so it was quite surprising that I told Russell about it.

Unknown to me, Russell was quite interested in the supernatural and took the story seriously. Being the sort of boy he was, he wanted to know more. In fact, he almost immediately suggested that the two of us should pay a visit – by night.

THE NO HOPER

I was appalled. How could we do that? Our parents would not allow us out after dark. No, he agreed. But what was to stop us sneaking out without them knowing?

It would, I suppose, be more difficult today, with 11 or 12-year-olds allowed to stay up much later than we were then. I was put to bed around 8pm and was expected to be asleep by nine at the latest. I wasn't, of course, but my parents did not know about the hours I spent reading with a torch under the bed clothes.

Russell's plan was simple. We would pretend to be asleep, get dressed and sneak out of the house around nine. We would then meet up and then set off on the 15-minute walk to Thorneyholme. In my case it would mean creeping passed the living room door, which was at the bottom of the stairs, but if my parents had the radio on, which they usually did, they would not hear me. A similar situation existed at his house.

So I agreed to the plan and in due course we put it into action. Everything went well and soon we were meeting up at the top of Adam's Hill and hurrying off on the same route I used every day on my way to school. There were few people about and none that seemed to think it unusual to see two boys out at such an hour. It was not particularly dark as it was a clear night with a fairly full moon.

It seemed darker as we neared our destination because in those days Thorneyholme Drive – the residential road which led to both Woodside and Thorneyholme – had no street lights and there were houses on one side only. The other side was a field where Percy's horses were grazed. We both had torches, but dared not use them in case it drew attention to us.

Thorneyholme by moonlight did indeed look spooky. Once in the grounds, we did resort to our torches to find our way through what had once probably been beautiful gardens, but were now just a tangle of

THE NO HOPER

undergrowth. As we neared the house it began to take on a sinister appearance, a looming black structure set against the starlit sky.

Our torches picked out windows, most of them boarded up but others framed by shattered glass which glistened in the light of our torches. Within, there seemed to be an impenetrable darkness.

I'm not sure what we planned to do. Russell was probably thinking of climbing in through a window but I was beginning to regret leaving the warmth and comfort of my bed. As it happened there was an unexpected development that terrified both of us and decided our future course of action for us.

There was a sudden fluttering sound – possibly, I decided later, the wings of a bird – followed by a scraping noise from inside the building and then the sound of a ghostly human voice.

Neither Russell nor I were renowned for our athletic prowess but I swear we both set Olympic records as we fled the scene, crashing unseeing through undergrowth and bushes and not slowing down until we reached Mobberley Road – a good quarter of-a-mile away.

We both managed to sneak back into our respective bedrooms without our parents ever being aware we had been out.

As I have already said, I have never since heard of any stories of ghostly goings-on at Thorneyholme. But I did read reports in the Knutsford Guardian of vagrants sleeping in the deserted house and thieves breaking in to steal lead. I can only assume we disturbed either one or the other. I just hope we scared them as much as they scared us.

It was not too long after that Thorneyholme was demolished and its site disappeared under a housing estate.

THE NO HOPER

POP STARS

Despite Percy being a first rate organist and a more than able pianist, music was not taught during my time at Knutsford College, although it had been listed as an "extra" during earlier times.

In my early years, the daily hymn singing was accompanied at the piano by Richard Aldridge, who went on to combine music with a business career. When he left, Percy would sometimes play and sometimes we would sing unaccompanied.

Richard's younger brother, Geoff, was a fine boy soprano and was frequently called on to solo during hymn singing.

Inspired by him, I began to sing enthusiastically myself, so much so that I attracted the attention of Jimmy.

"You're singing quite well, Skentelbery," he said one morning. "We'll have to give you a solo one morning."

The idea horrified me. Knutsford College might have knocked most of my shyness out of me but there was no way I was going to sing a solo in front of the whole school. I never opened my mouth during singing again and, fortunately, Jimmy must have forgotten about his offer because he never mentioned it again.

However, somebody bought me a mouth organ for a present one Christmas and I found I could play it quite well.

Gary Lewis also brought a mouth organ to school and for a while the two of us became mini pop stars with fans among our fellow students.

I thought Gary was better than me and he certainly had a better mouth organ – in fact he insisted on calling it a harmonica.

But there was a pop song in the charts around that time called "Walking to Missouri" and I mastered it and acquired quite a following of boys who repeatedly asked me to play it.

Understandably this frustrated Gary who, while a better player with a better instrument, could not play "Walking to Missouri." We discussed it

THE NO HOPER

and I agreed with him that it was a complete mystery why my tune was so much more popular than anything he could play – or even other tunes I could play.

I wonder how many real pop stars have pondered similar mysteries over the years?

Although we did not receive formal music lessons during my time, the subject did occasionally crop up in "general knowledge" lessons which seemed to take place whenever a teacher couldn't think of anything else to teach us.

During one such lesson, Jimmy started asking the class to name composers whose name began with various letters of the alphabet.

Eventually he asked if anyone knew a composer whose name began with "L".

Several hands went up, including mine.

Some bright spark gave the answer Listz which was accepted and several others gave names which were ruled inadmissible because they were musicians rather than composers.

Eventually, mine was the only hand still up and Jimmy pointed to me.

"Livingstone" I said, confidently

Jimmy frowned. "Livingstone? What did he write?"

My reply caused great mirth in the class but did not please Jimmy.

"I tawt I taw a puddy tat," said I.

The record, by Mel Blanc, had been a big hit some time previously and the tune had been written by Billy May and one Alan Livingstone. So my answer had to be accepted.

My interest in pop music did not please my parents who – my mother being a qualified piano teacher – leaned more towards the classics. Indeed, my earliest favourites had been Gilbert and Sullivan pieces I heard through my parents' involvement with the operatic society.

So when I started spending my pocket money on records by Frankie Laine, Johnny Ray and Guy Mitchell, my dad in particular began to wonder what

THE NO HOPER

I was learning at this school he was spending a good part of his salary to send me to.

He told me: "It's a waste of money buying these records. You get fed up of them after a few weeks and never play them again.

"You'll grow out of it."

After a while I began to realise he was right, at least about me quickly getting fed up with the records I bought.

My musical tastes began to mature – but not towards the classics as he had hoped. I gradually became a jazz fan – and remain so to this day.

But I don't think Percy had anything to do with it, nor even Denis Leighton, with his knowledge of Jelly Roll Morton.

After leaving school, my interest in jazz grew and in 1956 I managed to get tickets to see the Stan Kenton Orchestra at Manchester's King's Hall, Belle Vue.

Bob Jackson wasn't really into jazz, but he didn't like to miss out on anything and came with me, accompanied by a mutual friend, John Hennelly, who was not an Old Boy, but deserves a mention in this story if only because he and I have remained close friends for around 70 years even though he isn't in the slightest interested in cricket.

In those days, Piccadilly had, rightly, gained the reputation of being Manchester's red light district. In fact my father's paper, the Evening Chronicle, had staged a "clean up Piccadilly" campaign which, judging by the incident I am about to describe, had clearly been unsuccessful.

The three of us had to walk across Piccadilly en route from Manchester Central railway station to Belle Vue.

We were walking three abreast when a highly rouged lady, old enough to be any of our mothers, stepped into our path and, making a bee-line for Bob, said: "Hello, dearie - how are you?"

Bob faltered in mid-stride, flushed, but politely replied: "Very well, thank you" and walked on. We Knutsford College Old Boys certainly knew our manners. The concert was great, but we spent much of the train journey home pondering why she had picked on Bob.

THE NO HOPER

Did he look the most affluent or the most randy?
Arising from my interest in jazz, I took up the guitar, some time after leaving school, although I never really mastered it. Around that time everybody seemed to be playing guitar and some were quite good. But because I wanted to play jazz rather than rock and pop, which is a good deal easier to play, I struggled. But thanks to Edward Atkinson's Dad, who provided the venue, I did play in public once - at a friend's 21st birthday party. Mr Atkinson was licensee of the Lord Eldon pub in Knutsford and the party was in the upstairs function room. I played in a trio consisting of piano, guitar and drums. We were playing the pop tunes of the day and I did not really enjoy it - particularly when some of the more inebriated members of the audience started throwing sandwiches around. I had to duck several times to avoid being hit by a flying ham sandwich

Next morning I returned to the pub to help the drummer pick up his kit and was horrified to find sodden sandwiches sticking to the walls, windows and even the ceiling. What Mr Atkinson must have thought of us I shudder to think - but neither I nor the other two members of the band had been involved. At least, that's my story and I'm sticking to it.

These days, you hear lots of stories of rock stars trashing hotel rooms or recording studios, but I was clearly not of that stuff. Largely as a result of that evening I decided that live gigs were not for me.

Edward, I hasten to add, in case anyone thinks he was involved in the sandwich throwing, was away in the Merchant Navy at the time.

CHARACTERS

Many characters passed through the portals of Knutsford College over the years, but none could have been more colourful than John Knott.

He was Head Boy from 1945 to 1948 and also chairman of the Old Boys Association for 17 years, until his death on April 19, 2019.

Nobody seems quite sure how he got to be chairman because there was no formal election so far as I know. But that was the sort of person John was – brash, outspoken, full of fun, fond of his drink and fond of the ladies.

My time at Knutsford College overlapped only briefly with his, so I have few memories of him as a pupil. But my daily walk to school followed the same route as his so I frequently walked to school with him, and Richard and Geoffrey Aldridge, who were near neighbours of his. John and Richard were older than me but Geoff was about my age.

To me, John and Richard seemed like grown men. In fact, John was about four years older than me, but at that age, four years is a long time.

The conversation as we walked to school would be dominated by John – that was the sort of person he was, even at that age.

After leaving school he became an auctioneer - in fact one of the best known and most respected auctioneers in the North West.

Completely by chance, I saw quite a lot of him after I left school and joined the Knutsford Guardian as a junior reporter.

Les Groves, the chief reporter, was a close friend of John's so our former head boy was a frequent visitor to the Guardian office in King Street. As a result, I heard in graphic detail a lot about their adventures together as they travelled far and wide across Cheshire and the North West, usually in pursuit of the opposite sex.

It seemed they had one firm rule – if you wanted to paint the town red you painted some other town – not your own. I was now, of course, much older

THE NO HOPER

and wiser than the timid youth who had arrived at Knutsford College around the time John was leaving, but I was still in awe of some of the stories I heard.

Suffice to say they were not the sort of story I was expected to write for the Knutsford Guardian and not the sort of story to be repeated here. I heard most of them from Les , rather than John, and it may be that some journalistic licence came into play.

But if they were true – and at that age I was still probably gullible enough to believe almost anything – they seemed to put the rakish adventures the great lotharios of history, such as Don Juan, Casanova and Lord Byron, very much in the shade.

Some were just funny, however and a couple of them can be told here.

On one occasion, John was walking alone in the fields near Booth's Lake, carrying a stick he had picked up along the way. He saw a couple of ramblers approaching from the opposite direction – a man and his wife and their brutish looking dog.

The man was wearing shorts which revealed he had long, spindly legs with knobbly knees.

John looked pleasantly at the dog but the brute – I'm not sure what type it was, but it was big – glared back at him.

Suddenly the animal leapt at him, snarling, baring its teeth and aiming straight for a sensitive part of his anatomy which, given the pastimes we have already referred to, was rather precious to him.

"Jesus Christ!" he screamed, trying to leap out of the dog's way.

"Can't you keep your bloody dog under control?"

The rambler grabbed his dog by the neck and tried to drag it away from John, who was staggering around in a state of shock.

"I'm awfully sorry. He doesn't usually attack strangers."

John' response was typical of him: "You mean he usually only attacks people he knows!"

"Oh no – he doesn't normally attack anyone."

THE NO HOPER

"Well, why did he suddenly break the habit of a bloody lifetime when I came along?

"I think perhaps it was because you were carrying a stick," the dog's owner suggested.

"What! Do you mean he only attacks bloody cripples?"

"There's no need to be like that. Don't you know there's a lady present?"

John tried to calm down but failed.

"I'm afraid I was too busy trying to protect myself from your bloody tripe-hound to notice who was here. But, quite frankly, I wouldn't care if the Archbishop of Canterbury was present if your animal behaved like that.

"Keep the bloody creature on a lead in future."

The rambler stuttered: "I think you are over-reacting..."

But John was now walking away.

A few yards away, however, he turned and shouted: "What's more, if I had legs like yours the last thing I would do is wear bloody shorts."

The man was speechless but his dog, apparently sensing that his owner had been insulted, calmly walked over to a tree stump which John had been thinking of sitting on and urinated on it.

Well, of course, none of all that happened. I just made it up, hoping it might make you laugh, shamelessly stealing the idea from a book by Bill Bryson, to whom I sincerely apologise.

But I like to think that is how John would have reacted in such a situation.

Another story about him that IS true concerns a night when John and Les Groves went to the Marcliff cinema in Knutsford.

In those days, cinemas always played the National Anthem at the end of a performance and the audience was expected to stand.

John, Les and the whole audience did so, but one man started to walk up the centre aisle, heading for the exit, while the anthem was still playing.

John, who was nothing if not patriotic, leapt out in front of him and hissed: "Stand still you yob. Have you no respect for the Crown?"

The miscreant paused, swung a punch at John, knocking him back into his seat, and walked on out.

THE NO HOPER

On another occasion, John and Les went out for a night in John's father's brand new car. On the homeward journey John managed to drive it off the road and turn it over in a field. Neither of them were seriously injured although Les was taken to hospital with a head wound that required stitches.

This meant he had to have the top of his head shaved, which left him looking like a Franciscan monk.

John's reaction was to send him a get-well card addressed to "Brother Groves, The Cloisters, Sandileigh Avenue. Knutsford." The postman managed to deliver it the right house.

Eventually, John grew out of the outrageous years of his young adulthood. He was involved in a tragic road accident which may have changed him. But in subsequent years he put his natural skills to good use, raising money for good causes and was eventually awarded the MBE for his services to charity.

Another Head Boy who was something of a character was Barry Cooper. In fact, I don't recall the school ever having another Head Boy after he left, some time before the eventual closure.

I didn't know Barry too well at school but got to know him well in later years when we both lived in the Warrington area, where he became a successful businessman.

After running a string of corner shops, he founded a coach business and for many years was the main coach operator in Warrington. He had a fleet of luxury coaches all bearing his name "Barry Cooper Coaches."

I bumped into him occasionally during an eight year period when I worked as the Warrington district reporter for the Lancashire Evening Post

Then in 1968 I decided to start my own business in freelance journalism and publishing. Warrington had been designated a "New Town" and work started on expanding an old, industrial town famed for wire, soap, beer and Rugby League. I decided the time was ripe to give the town its own magazine – a glossy quarterly which I called "New Warrington."

THE NO HOPER

I left the Evenng Post to run this magazine alongside freelancing for various regional and national newspapers and also helping in an art and craft shop my wife, Patricia, had opened.
I mistakenly thought the Warrington New Town concept would prove popular with the local population and that my magazine would benefit from being associated, unofficially, with the newly formed New Town Development Corporation.
Calling on the "old boys' network" I asked Barry to advertise with me and he generously agreed to do so. He advertised regularly with me throughout the eight year life of the magazine.
Unfortunately not too many other local people gave such loyal support because they thought it was linked to the unpopular development corporation. Even when I dropped the word "New" from the title and it became simply "The Warrington Magazine" sales were disappointing. I eventually ceased publishing the magazine to concentrate on my freelance work, which fortunately prospered.
One thing I admired about Barry was that whenever I called at his depot, he would invariably be under a coach, in overalls, with a spanner in his hand. Although he employed quite a large staff, he remained "hands on."
Eventually he sold out to a major company from Manchester and retired to the Isle of Man, apparently after a disagreement with the Inland Revenue.

Another notable character during my time was John White, an excellent all-round sportsman.
His father ran a long-established sports shop in Warrington town centre. It had, I think, been established by John's grandfather, also named John. After leaving school, John worked in the business, eventually taking it over from his father in partnership with his brother Paul.
The business still traded under the name "John White" and when it finally closed gained national publicity as "the oldest sports shop in the world".
As it happened, as my wife and I climbed the property ladder, we moved to the village of Croft, near Warrington where John lived with his wife,

THE NO HOPER

Maureen. As a result my son Gary went to school with John's sons and got to know them well – particularly his son, Nick, who later briefly worked in our business as an advertising executive.

He used to sit near me and it seemed strange to hear his voice in the next room as he sounded just like his father.

One consequence of John and I living in the same village was that our wives got to know one another.

After exchanging schoolboy stories they had heard from John and I they both came to the conclusion that we had been to some sort of institution for backward boys.

When John sadly died in 2009 Nick gave a moving eulogy at the packed funeral during which he described what it was like to walk around Warrington with his father.

"It seemed everyone knew him," he said.

Doug Griffiths was another Head Boy, although he left the school shortly afterwards so held the position only briefly.

I became friendly with him because we both liked science fiction and we used to swap paperback books.

As a day boy, I was able to go in the local newsagents and spot the new books as they came out and then pass the word on to Doug.

Now, of course, Doug is the editor and owner of the Knutsford College Old Boys Association website.

He has spent hours and travelled miles in compiling a fascinating history of the college which attracts visitors from all over the world, meeting up with many former students and their families and adding their stories to the website.

Doug came from a farming family, although he did not pursue agriculture after leaving school, preferring a career in the RAF.

He was particularly friendly with John White and sometimes they would meet up in the summer holidays, John cycling to the Griffiths farm at Peover. On one occasion it was harvest time and the pair were helping

THE NO HOPER

on a cart stacking sheaves of corn to take half-a-mile down the road to the farm.
Doug recalls that day well: "John had somehow pinched one of the bottles of cider my Dad kept for the men. On the journey to the farm we sat on top of the load of corn, knocking back the cider.
"By the time we arrived at the farm we were more than a little light headed and slid off the side of the cart - luckily onto the grass verge.
"John looked at me and said: 'Hell, Doug, we nearly went under the wheels – let's get out of here quick.'" They did, and no one seemed to miss them
The pair went to a nearby lake where a unit of General "Blood and Guts" Patten's U.S. Army had been training. They had apparently left some rowing boats there.
"We pinched one of the boats and practised some rowing to keep out of the way", said Doug. "But John started rocking the boat, fell in the lake and disappeared.
"When he came up, the first thing he said was: 'I think I've lost two bob'". For the benefit of younger readers, that's 20 pence.

Neville Kaye sticks in my memory for many reasons but particularly because we were close friends. He was an outstanding sportsman – he and I spent hours playing cricket on Knutsford Heath and later at Knutsford Cricket Club. After marrying and leaving Knutsford he played at Alderley Edge, one of the leading clubs in Cheshire.
I have already mentioned his remarkable ability to speak in belches and also the farting contests he initiated. These involved farting as many times as possible within a given time scale. Extra points could be awarded for volume, longevity and odour.
Those involved were rumoured to "train" on Andrew's Liver Salts!
Neville's parents ran a confectionary business in Princess Street, Knutsford and he always cycled home for his lunch. I didn't know it at the

THE NO HOPER

time, but he would frequently return in the afternoon with loads of cakes which he would distribute to hungry boarders.

Doug Griffiths says he first sampled Eccles Cakes thanks to Neville – and they have remained a favourite of his ever since.

Whether Mr Kaye knew that his cakes were being taken to feed starving youngsters I can't say.

Tony Banfield had a unique record among Knutsford College students. His mother, then Pam Murray, was one of only four girls to have attended the school so he became the only student to have followed in his mother's footsteps to attend the school. She was a pupil around the time it opened in 1927.

Boarders were regularly drafted in to carry out tasks such as mowing the lawn, rolling the cricket pitch, shovelling coke for the boiler, etc.

Michael Burke told an amusing story of how he and his friend Stanley Eden were given the task of brushing up needles which had fallen from the cedar trees.

They worked together, collecting several wheelbarrow loads before finally getting bored and starting to duel using their shovels as swords. It was all playful and in good fun until Michael's "sword" accidentally caught Stanley in the face – right between the eyes.

It only caused a small wound, but it bled profusely so the pair went to the Matron Maria Maude. She panicked and screamed for Percy who in turn called for Jimmy, who patched up Stanley with a small zinc plaster.

Percy could not be convinced that the injury had occurred accidentally. He lectured Michael for almost an hour.

"Disputes are to be settled in the gymnasium with boxing gloves, not fought out in malice with deadly weapons," he said. He could not be made to understand that there had been no dispute, just some horseplay that had gone wrong. However, he cooled down eventually and Michael escaped

THE NO HOPER

punishment. The two boys were rather amused later when they were made to shake hands before the assembled school and "make up".
Some months later, however. Percy gave Michael six lashes with the cane – for something he could not even remember.

Karl Smith spent four years at Knutsford College almost by accident, as it were.
His elder brother was due to start at the school at the start of the next term and the family – Karl, his brother and their mother and father – arrived to meet Percy and look the place over.
A member of staff took his brother off for a tour of the college and, afterwards, the family went out to their car to go home. But his brother had apparently seen more than enough – he announced that he'd decided he didn't like it and wanted to go home. All rather embarrassing for his Mum and Dad, who weren't quite sure what to do.
Karl saved the day by saying: "Dad, can I go instead?"
A relieved father replied: "Of course you can son" – and so began Karl's education at Knutsford College.

Max Price was a great character - not just in his own right but also because of his father who seemed to me to be the sort of father every boy should have. The Price family lived in Garden Road, a few doors away from Knutsford Motors - a main Ford dealer - who had a large concrete forecourt which of an evening and at weekends provided a superb surface for roller skating. A crowd of us would descend on it to play roller hockey - Max, Neville Kaye, Bob Jackson, Edward Atkinson, myself and others who were not students at the college.
Max's Dad was a superb roller skater and would often come out and join in - and the team that had him as a member would invariably win. One day my mother met Mrs Price while out shopping and got chatting, as mothers do. My Mum was highly amused to hear from Mrs Price that group of us had called and asked if Max could come out to play. On being told that

THE NO HOPER

Max had been "grounded" for some misdemeanour we apparently asked: "Well, can Mr Price come out then?" And he did!
On another occasion a group of us were invited into the back garden at the Price home to see a demonstration of a cannon that Max and his Dad had built. We were all told to stand back and the cannon was fired, sending a ball-bearing across the garden to take a hefty chunk out of a brick wall! What "Health and Safety" would make of it these days, I shudder to think.
After leaving school, Max embarked on a successful career in the Merchant Navy.

THE DELAMERE RUNNER

The village of Delamere lies some 15 miles from Knutsford. It is most famous for its forest which today is ranked among the leading tourist attractions in the North West of England. It also boasts a lake and is renowned as a high class residential area which attracts the county set.

Even in the late 1940s it must have been popular among the upper middle classes because a number of the "sons of gentlemen" who attended Knutsford College hailed from there. They would have been boarders as in those days even well-heeled, car-owning parents would have regarded 15 miles as being too far to take their sons to school daily. They were probably weekly boarders rather than termly boarders, but boarders they would be.

So it was not surprising that Delamere would crop up in conversation from time to time.

It meant nothing to me, of course. I knew a mere was a lake and that were quite a lot of them in Cheshire. I knew about Mere, which was about three miles outside Knutsford. For some reason, I thought that Knutsford Moor, which lay about half way between my home and the school, was also known as "the mere". Perhaps it was, but not by the pupils of Knutsford College.

At any rate, somehow or other a conversation started about how long it would take for our Delamere students to get home on foot. Perhaps one or more of them were planning to abscond, possibly driven by the pangs of hunger, because boarders were not exactly well fed.

The general view was that the distance involved was too great to attempt on foot...until I piped up with: "Delamere? That's not far - I ran there once."

At first my casual remark was greeted by a stunned silence. But this quickly turned to ridicule as my fellow pupils grasped the significance of what I had said and realised, quite correctly, that it could not be true.

THE NO HOPER

One or two of my closer friends suggested, kindly, that I must be confusing Delamere with some other place. I was not, after all, regarded as one of the school's best athletes.

But I was adamant. I was not confused, nor was my knowledge of local geography in any way deficient. I had run to Delamere, with a friend (who was conveniently not a pupil at Knutsford College) and, what's more, it had not taken us very long.

Pressed as to how long, exactly, I began to warm to my subject, and draw on my imagination. It was some time ago, I said, but I was sure it had only been a couple of hours.

The derision each of my claims attracted grew in ferocity. Muttered ridicule swiftly became a clamour and then an uproar.

Other boys arrived on the scene, heard of my claims and joined in a growing demand that I provide proof. My friends began to desert me until only one - Max Price, who was a year or two older than me - stuck by me, although even he was insisting that I must be mistaken and that I had in fact run somewhere else. I stuck to my story, having gone too far to back down.

OK, I finally said, I would prove it - if they could come up with a way in which I could do so.

After some discussion, it was decided that I would have to run round the school grounds continuously until it was judged I had run far enough. The school's grounds were expansive, but even so it was agreed - by them, not me - that it would take several hundred circuits before I could be said to have proved my point.

Some distrusting soul pointed out that it would be possible for me to cheat by stopping running once I was out of sight, but a solution was quickly found. I would be accompanied by other boys, in relays, who would ensure that I kept running. At least two boys would run with me on each lap to make it less likely that I could bribe my way out of the situation I had talked myself into.

THE NO HOPER

And so the ordeal began. A route was agreed that would take me and my "escorts" through the courtyard, along the Cedar Drive, around the cricket field, through the woods to the football field, along the bottom path, passed the Lone Pine and back passed the front entrance of the school and back to the courtyard. At this point, my escorts would change and I would start my second lap.

The first lap started with plenty of laughter and chatter until one of my escorts, Anthony Brighouse, suggested that if we were to complete the challenge we should save our breath by not talking. I agreed to this rather too readily for someone capable of running to Delamere!

Lap 1 was completed without too much difficulty, although no speed records were broken. The relief escorts took over and Lap 2 was also completed. By this time, most of the volunteer escorts had become bored with the whole project and had disappeared, so the two boys who had done the first lap were persuaded to tackle Lap 3. No-one seemed to notice that while these arrangements were being made we had stopped, thus giving me some breathing space.

The third lap started but we had hardly gone 100 yards before we ran out of time - the bell sounded announcing the end of the lunchtime break.

No-one had apparently given any thought to the obvious problem of how we could complete such a challenge in the time available. Unless it was that none of my colleagues thought I would be unable to complete even three laps!

That was the end of it. No-one ever suggested re-starting the challenge. But it would be wrong to say the matter was forgotten as for months afterwards I had to live with a new nickname - "The Delamere Runner."

Privately, I admitted to Max Price that perhaps I had been mistaken and that probably the place I had run to was Knutsford Moor.

Actually I can't remember even running there.

THE NO HOPER

CONKERS AND MARBLES

They were not, I am afraid, very much appreciated at the time, but the grounds of Knutsford College were a veritable heaven for a schoolboy. They were about 14 acres and in addition to the cricket field, the football field and the lower part of the football field, near the Bottom Path, which was later used as another cricket field, there were extensive woodlands, a large lawn which for brief periods included a grass tennis court, the Cedar Drive, the terrace, a cobbled courtyard, a walled kitchen garden and another field which during my time at the school was unused other than for grazing Percy's horses.

They were all very much taken for granted but they contributed very much to school life. There were cedar trees, not just along the Cedar Drive but scattered elsewhere in the woods. There were horse chestnut trees, which provided the ammunition for the annual conker fighting season and there were chestnut trees which, in my case, were a source of additional refreshment to school dinners. I also used to collect them and take them home where I would roast them on a shovel over the fire. Absolutely delicious. Even my Mum and Grandma enjoyed them.

The woods provided adventure playgrounds that most children today could only dream of. We did not, I am afraid, value them as we should have done. I have already described how new boys would be hurled headlong through holly bushes. It didn't do the boys much harm but it must have caused considerable damage to the bushes.

The cedar trees could give off a resin which could, with a little patience and a plentiful supply of matches, be set alight. Many a time I can remember seeing flames leaping several feet up the trunk of one of these magnificent trees. Often the perpetrators of such vandalism would flee in fright, leaving the tree ablaze. I don't recall anyone ever being reprimanded for these acts of arson, nor any outbreak of fire getting out of hand. Somebody must have always been around to extinguish the flames and the trees never seemed to suffer any permanent damage.

THE NO HOPER

Conker battles were the main breaktime occupation in the Autumn. It started with the gathering of the conkers and few boys would wait for them to fall. Huge branches were hurled up into the trees to dislodge the horse chestnuts hanging there.

The battles inevitably took place on the Cedar Drive or the cricket field and were fought to the usual rules of conker fighting.

A new conker would become a "oncer" when it defeated another conker. If it won again it would become a "twicer" and so on. If a twicer defeated another twicer it would become a "fourer". A "fiver" which defeated another "fiver" would become a "tenner".

Just how honest my fellow students were in keeping a tally on their conkers' scores I don't know, but in this respect I suspect most were honourable.

Of course there were ways of making your conker tougher. Baking them in an oven was the best known - a ploy more readily available to day boys as the boarders would have found it difficult getting access to an oven. Another toughening process was soaking the conker in vinegar, although I was never convinced that this made much difference. Of course you could bake a conker AND soak it in vinegar, which probably left the oven with a rather pungent smell.

I had one such conker which acquired a three figure record which I was determined not to lose to any other boy. I kept it at home and every time I acquired another conker with a reasonable tally I would take that home too, tie it on to my mother's washing line and then attack it with the "super conker". By such means I added to the super conker's impressive record.

During the winter, conkers wars were replaced with snowball battles - often day boys versus borders.

As day boys and boarders dined separately, each "army" would have half the mid-day break to roam the grounds without interference from the other.

I remember one winter when the snow was thick on the ground for what seemed like weeks on end. We day boys made and stockpiled a huge

THE NO HOPER

number of snowballs in the woods near the Bottom Path in readiness for when the boarders spilled out of the dining room after dinner.

They must have had an idea where our stockpile was, however, because they came straight for it and a battle of titanic proportions took place as we tried to prevent them reaching our stockpile and turning it against us. Some of the snowballs had been made several days previously and had been turned into lumps of ice by overnight frost. They were pretty lethal missiles. Others were soft and flaky and burst when hurled through the undergrowth at the advancing boarders, showering them with wet snow.

Just what the outcome of this battle was I do not recall - but a lot of boys sat in that afternoon's lessons in soaking wet clothes.

In the summer, it was the marble season and again the venue was the Cedar Drive. Over the years, a number of small holes had been created on either side of the drive and these were used by the marble players in much the same way as golf is played. The winner was the player who got his marble into the hole with the least number of tries. If the game was "for keeps" the loser would lose his marble although there was a ready market in swaps and exchanges by which lost marbles could find their way back into the original owner's hands.

THE NO HOPER

SHIP AHOY!

Today, much of the site of Knutsford College is a housing estate. But in the days when the college was there - and indeed for some years afterwards - the school building stood on the very edge of the developed area of Over Knutsford.

Manor Park Road - a country lane with only a handful of large houses on it and now split into two roads, Manor Park North and Manor Park South - separated the school grounds from open fields across which there was a footpath which led to Booth's Lake.

The lake, of course, was out of bounds officially. But unofficially it was frequently visited by errant groups of boys, during the lunch break and, for boarders, at the weekends also. Many were the adventures which took place on and around Booth's Lake.

As a day boy, I took part in few of them, but one in particular involved a group of four - myself, Bob Jackson, Brian Southern and David Sands.

We set off after lunch and ventured farther around the lake than I, for one, had ever done before. Eventually we came to what was clearly a boathouse and on gaining entry discovered a rowing boat.

It was a simple matter to open the insecure gate which led to a short channel leading to the open lake and all sorts of possibilities presented themselves. There were no oars in the boat - presumably the owners thought this would render it unusable to trespassers.

But they had reckoned without the ingenuity of Knutsford College students. We found some fallen branches beneath a nearby tree and reckoned we could use them to paddle the boat out on to the lake. We had less than an hour before we were due back in school, but time meant little to us. We all embarked and began to paddle the boat out into the open water.

Four pairs of willing hands got to work, two of us paddling on one side and two on the other. I had recently been reading some of Arthur Ransome's "Swallows and Amazons" books, so considered myself

THE NO HOPER

something of an expert on matters to do with small boats. There was much talk of "port" and "starboard" and "forr'd" and "aft" and even the occasional "shiver me timbers."

The fictional lake in Arthur Ransome's stories had several islands and our lake had one too. I think we all had our hearts set on reaching this island and exploring it. We paddled like windmills and the boat surged towards the centre of the lake.

What we had failed to take account of was the wind, which as we got further out from the shore, strengthened considerably. Soon we were heading for the island at a fair rate of knots!

It was then that one of us - I can't remember who, but he must have boasted a wristwatch - suddenly thought of the time.

Brian Southern, who was a bit more sensible than the rest of us, said: "We had better turn back - now we know about the boat we can always come again."

There was some argument, but eventually it was agreed that we should paddle back to the boathouse while there was still an outside chance of us getting back to school in time for the afternoon assembly and roll-call.

Drawing on my vast knowledge of seamanship, gleaned from "Swallows and Amazons", I explained the principle of rowing on one side and backwatering on the other to turn the boat around.

This we achieved without too much difficulty - but then our problems started.

Paddle as we might, we could not make any headway against the wind, which was steadily carrying us further and further away from the boathouse. We paddled like maniacs but to no avail. All we were able to do was set the boat on a somewhat wayward course back towards the centre of the lake.

Then, to our horror, we found ourselves being carried towards an area of reeds and visions of us being trapped in all-enveloping and clinging vegetation came to my mind. I seemed to remember one of Mr Ransome's

THE NO HOPER

books describing how ships became trapped in the Sargasso Sea, their crews perishing from lack of food and water.

In fact the reed bed was our salvation. As the boat entered it we saw something floating - trapped by the reeds. It was an oar.

David Sands leaned out of the boat, the rest of us hanging on to his legs, and managed to grab it and pull it aboard.

Then he rowed like a madman on one side while the rest of us paddled like mad with the branches on the other. This enabled us to steer a somewhat erratic course back to the boathouse.

There were some hasty attempts made to cover our tracks. The boat was tied up inside the boathouse exactly as it had been before. The doors were closed and our tree branch paddles thrown away. Then we fled across the fields back to school, arriving back breathless but just in time for assembly.

Whether or not the owners of the boat ever knew it had been "borrowed" by schoolboy pirates I don't know. They may have been puzzled at the reappearance of an oar they had presumably thought lost. Again I don't know.

The four of us never returned to resume our voyage of discovery. I did return to the boathouse on a later occasion with Bob Jackson but found the boat was no longer there.

In fact, Bob and I visited Booth's Lake on many occasions, at the weekends, in school holidays and on games days in the winter when neither of us wanted to play football and found that we could slip away unnoticed.

This was for the purpose of sailing home-made model yachts attached to balls of string to ensure we didn't lose them.

One such outing resulted in an encounter with a water bailif who thought we were fishing. But once he realised we were not he was quite happy to let us continue.

Looking back on it, whoever owned Booth's Hall around this time, was quite relaxed about people straying on to their land.

THE NO HOPER

There were many footpaths regularly used by the public and most of them leading to the lake. One winter – again, it may have been 1947 because, according to the Met Office, the February of that year was the coldest on record at that time – the lake was frozen solid for several weeks.

Neville Kaye and I taught ourselves to skate that winter – in my case using a pair of skates screwed to my football boots. We went every Saturday and Sunday – and it seemed to me that half the population of Knutsford went too. Impromptu ice hockey matches were played in the centre of the lake, the players using everything from hockey sticks to walking sticks. Skating even went on after dark, with cars parked alongside the lake with their headlights trained on the ice. Neville and I were still going days after a gradual thaw set in and skated all over the lake listening to the ice cracking beneath us. We just skated faster in case the ice collapsed. Eventually, of course, it did - and guess who happened to be skating over it when it did.

What happened was that I over-balanced and fell backwards on my bum, creating a bum-shaped hole in the ice into which I fitted perfectly. I plugged that hole as efficiently as any cork ever fitted a bottle, with my legs and arms sticking upwards. I was, in fact, stuck. Neville, at considerable risk to himself, approached cautiously and held out a stick which I was able to grab. He then pulled me clear of the hole which fortunately was quite close to dry land.

I suppose I should, as I waddled miserably home with a cold and wet bum, have thanked Neville for rescuing me. But he came out with joke about a passing fish thinking my end had been in sight, so I didn't. When I got home and my parents discovered what had happened, I was banned from skating on the lake again.

I cannot vouch for another story told about the fields around Booth's Lake, although I have heard it from several sources.

A party of boarders were taken on a walk one weekend by Denis Leighton. Some were ahead of the rest of the party and came across a used condom, lying in the grass.

THE NO HOPER

Of course these worldly-wise students knew full-well what it was, but ran to Denis with cries of "Please sir, what is this?"
Denis, without batting an eyelid, explained that it was a meteorological balloon that had malfunctioned and that they should keep well away from it in case in contained dangerous chemicals!

THE GUNPOWDER PLOT

Some things stick in your mind for no apparent reasons. Others because they were pretty dramatic at the time.

One such involved my friend Bob Jackson and I one November – and resulted in us being suspected of attempted arson by a good proportion of the townspeople of Knutsford!

I'm not sure how it came about but for some reason the two of us were in First Class room on our own during "Prep" – the hour long session between 4pm, when the school day officially ended – and 5pm when day boys were sent home. This period was when we were supposed to do work in preparation for the following day and, as a result of this, we were never set homework.

The boarders did their "prep" later, after the day boys had left.

It was early November and we had already started collecting fireworks in readiness for Guy Fawkes Night, although I doubt if we were supposed to have them with us at school.

Safety seemed to be much less of an issue in those days. Bangers were louder than they are today, sparklers really did sparkle and a Roman Candle in the hands of a daring schoolboy became a lethal weapon. Looking back, I am amazed that there were not dozens of fatalities or serious injuries every year.

I can't recall whether I had any fireworks with me that day but Bob certainly did.

It must have been getting near 5pm and we had probably finished our "prep" so Bob decided it was a good time to experiment with fireworks.

There was a coal fire in the classroom and he decided to extract some powder from a firework and throw it in the fire.

He did this several times and, of course, the powder flared up. But not enough to satisfy Bob.

THE NO HOPER

I was actually on the other side of the room, some distance from the fireplace, when I saw him lean forward to empty powder from the firework directly into the flames.

"Hey – you'd better be careful," I said.

But I had hardly uttered the warning when the powder began to pour into the fire. Flames leapt up and ignited the powder that was still inside the firework.

Bob reeled backwards with the firework still clutched in his hand.

His arm described a graceful arc above his head, the fountain of fire shooting up to the ceiling and tracing a burn mark along the ceiling paper.

There then followed a mighty explosion that shook the very building.

There was a blinding white light that left me stunned and unable to see very much. What happened to Bob I don't know.

When my eyesight recovered I saw the room was full of dense smoke. But I could see no sign of Bob and thought perhaps he had managed to get out through the door into the hall way.

Whatever, I decided it was time for me to get out too.

I was still partly blinded and blundered out into the darkened hall only to collide with the diminutive figure of Miss Dick – the elderly lady who taught Third Class.

She appeared to be in a state of shock and I clearly remember her saying: "What is it? What are they moving in there?"

Well, as far as I was concerned, the thing I was moving was myself – as quickly and as far away as possible.

But I was still blundering about in the semi-darkness and still had no idea what had happened to Bob

Then David Wrigley appeared on the scene, charged into the smoke-filled classroom and emerged moments later leading a confused-looking Bob, who was clutching his wrist.

I heard Mr Wrigley say: "You stupid boy" and saw him leading him up the stairs in the direction of the head's study.

THE NO HOPER

I hung around for a while, without seeing either of them, or Miss Dick, again and eventually decided it was time I went home.

Whether or not I told my parents what had happened when I got home, I can't remember.

But next day I learned that Bob had been taken to hospital with a badly burned wrist. The day after I went to see him at his home and found him in his usual, cheerful mood. He was, after all, going to get a few days off school.

When the Knutsford Guardian came out that weekend, it reported that there had been no serious accidents on Guy Fawkes Night but that there had been an incident at Knutsford College when a boy had suffered "minor burns" while experimenting with fireworks.

The Knutsford rumour-mill soon got to work however and my mother was shocked to learn from a friend that Bob and I had been trying to blow up the school!

THE SECRET DEN

Woodside, the stately home which housed Knutsford College was a magnificent building. It was not Listed as a building of historic or architectural interest but I strongly suspect that if it still stood today it would be.

Its imposing exterior was matched by equally impressive rooms inside, particularly the hall with a fine staircase leading to the upper floors which were, to day boys anyway, pretty well forbidden territory. Boarders probably knew those floors well, as the dormitories were there. But even they used a different staircase – one which had probably been used by the servants in previous times.

There were cellars, of course, and beneath them the foundations which extended beneath the whole building.

These areas were strictly "out of bounds" but this did not deter the bolder students from sneaking down to explore. I even ventured down myself, once, but chickened out when confronted by low, inky black corridors. Others were braver souls and there was a legend that one boy got lost in the foundations and found himself beneath the First Class room during assembly, when the register was being called.

According to the story, when his name was called out he replied from the depths below and the master taking the register didn't notice that the boy's voice was somewhat muffled. Realising where he was, the youngster was able to find his way back to the steps leading down from the ground floor and get back to his classroom before he was missed. Whether this happened, or whether it is just a legend I cannot say, but there was certainly a small hole in the classroom floor which would have enabled the boy's voice to be heard.

There was another story about that hole which told how a boy – believed to be John Egerton - set fire to a small piece of paper and dropped it through the hole. Flames could be seen in the blackness below but

THE NO HOPER

eventually they went out, much to the relief of the boys attending a scripture lesson in the room above.

Another version of the story told how John excused himself to go to the toilet, sneaked down into the cellars, extinguished the fire and got back to the classroom without being caught.

Whichever version is true, had that little fire not gone out, there could easily have been a major blaze that would have made Bob Jackson's firework experiments seem pretty small beer.

But the best story about the network of corridors and passageways below the school concerns "the den."

It seems to have all started with Peter Chadwick, a pupil with an interest in telephonic communications. He read in some boys' magazine how you could make a simple "telephone" using two tin cans and a length of taut string.

The idea was that you could create a vibratory effect which would enable two people to talk to each other.

Peter was in a small dormitory, housing only five boys, and some distance from the other, larger dormitories and he reasoned that it would be possible to talk to his friend, Trevor Jarvis, who was in one of the other dormitories – in fact the only one where it was possible to stretch the tin can "telephone" in a straight line.

Just how successful this was is not clear. But it must have worked to some extent because Trevor found himself having to relay messages between various boys in the two dormitories and got fed up with acting as a "telephone exchange"

Peter, however, was now gripped with the idea of becoming a telephone engineer. He persuaded a small group of boys to join him in a more ambitious project - building a den in the foundations. It was accessed via a trapdoor in the cellar and according to those boys who knew about it, was a highly sophisticated installation for its day

It had electric lighting and a communication system linking it to the student common room.

THE NO HOPER

This intercom enabled conversation between the den and the library in the common room. Three specific books concealed the speaker and microphone.

Close by Woodside, as we have already discussed, was the even larger former stately home, Thorneyholme, which had been commandeered by the US Army during the war. After they departed – no doubt to take part in the D Day landings – it was left in an advanced state of dereliction. It was frequently visited by vagrants and groups of students – mostly boarders, I think - on clandestine expeditions outside the college grounds.

There was no shortage of wiring in the old building and some of this was "borrowed" for lighting and the intercom system in the den.

All the necessary equipment for the intercom was available except for the microphone. There was no way one could be purchased, given the meagre amount of pocket money given even to the "sons of gentlemen" in those times – even if one had been available to buy.

Speaking many years later, as an adult, Peter said: "I am sorry to this day that desire overcame honesty and we figured out that we could steal one. I am ashamed to say that we stole it in the dead of night from the telephone in the booth on the corner across from the Legh Arms. It worked like a charm."

Ironically, the Legh Arms was the pub where Percy and Jimmy spent much of their leisure time!

Few day boys were allowed to see the secret den but, predictably, John Knott was one who did.

It impressed him greatly and years later he was still enthralling wide-eyed audiences with descriptions of a comfortable refuge for boys, well stocked with food and drink so that youngsters still hungry after the less than generous meals served up by the college, need never go hungry.

Apparently there was a second cellar which could be entered from the kitchen.

This contained a large, commercial-style refrigerator with four doors behind which were sections where butter, milk, cheese and other

THE NO HOPER

perishable goods were kept. Beneath this, a flight of steps led down to a lower level where dry stores were kept. This was sealed off to prevent hungry students from raiding the stores at night.

Needless to say these defences were frequently breached so it is likely the food stored in the den originated from the kitchen.

There is a story that a teacher was in the common room one night, reprimanding some boys for noisy behaviour, when Peter, in the basement and not knowing he was there, chose that moment to put through a call. The teacher was startled to hear a disembodied voice coming from the book shelf, saying: "Is there any bugger there?"

Whoever the teacher was, he must have chosen to keep quiet about the intercom because he didn't report it to Percy.

But of course, the secret den was eventually discovered – during the summer holidays when the students were all away.

Percy was furious. How he knew Peter Chadwick was involved I don't know, but he did. Perhaps there was some incriminating evidence found in the den.

He telephoned his mother and informed her that Peter was expelled with immediate effect.

Mrs Chadwick was apparently a lady not easily intimidated. Her immediate response was to say: "Good – now I can send him to Sandbach Grammar."

Percy must have been somewhat taken aback by this and later called back to rescind his decision. Probably he had realised he would be losing a valuable portion of his income.

As a result Peter returned to the college – apparently somewhat reluctantly.

Years later he said: "The hullabaloo it created was incredible, but looking back I suppose it was justified.

"I think after that we confined ourselves to more mundane pastimes, such as marbles and conkers."

THE NO HOPER

While on the subject of Peter Chadwick, he and a friend of his, Tony Hill, laid claim to a unique record – that of being the only college students ever to venture into Knutsford of an evening dressed as women.

Given that they chose to do so when hundreds of American troops were based in and around the town, it was clearly rather a dangerous escapade.

The pair were among a small number of boarders who occasionally and for various reasons had to stay at the school during the summer holidays and they often got up to all sorts of tricks to relieve the boredom.

They were certainly not the only students to sneak out after "lights out" and the fact that Knutsford was out of bounds would not deter many. There are probably many untold stories of conduct unbecoming to the sons of gentlemen. But I doubt if anyone else went into town in drag!

The adventure must have been planned well in advance because Peter had borrowed his sister Pauline's clothes. They wore headscarves to hide their short hair.

It was 1944 and the town was swarming with US soldiers based in a large camp on Knutsford Heath. The pair received quite a few wolf whistles as they walked around town.

But according to Tony, the trickiest part of the venture was sneaking down the back stairs, passing the masters' common room to exit via a window in the main classroom.

Years later he said, "When you were as bored as we were nothing was too hot or heavy".

WHIZ KIDS

L to R Geoff Lomas, Trent Moreton and two friends

During my time at Knutsford College there was no science or technology taught – unless you count Jimmy's woodwork classes. But that did not mean we didn't have any technically minded boys – far from it.

We have already heard about Peter Chadwick's telecommunications wizardry down in the Woodside basement, but two other students who I considered to be whiz kids were Geoff Lomas – who was also a pretty sporty type – and Trent Moreton, who wore spectacles, was very studious and generally seemed to me to be a real intellect.

They were both a little older than me and both left school before the eventual closure. But I stayed in touch with them because Geoff's parents ran an electrical shop in Knutsford and both Geoff and Trent worked in the business for a time.

THE NO HOPER

I was a regular customer at the shop because it was the only place in Knutsford where you could buy records. They had a room at the back of the shop where you could browse through the records and even hear them in a sound-proof booth. This would have been pretty commonplace in Manchester, or even places like Altrincham and Northwich, but in Knutsford it was cutting-edge stuff.

Lomas's also had an electrical contracting business and I fancy this is where Geoff and Trent worked. I remember them telling me once that they were developing a video recorder – something which interested me very much because I was already into sound recording and cine films and the idea of being able to record both sound and pictures at the same time fascinated me. But one day I saw Geoff and asked him how the video project was going and he admitted they had given up the idea because "the BBC have beaten us to it."

Later on in this narrative you will hear of how Geoff set up a racing car company, but even at this stage in his career he was interested in car design.

One of the early "scoops" I was able to take to the Knutsford Guardian when I started there was a story about Geoff and Trent building their own car – presumably a kit-car. I went with a photographer to see the car put through its paces in Mere Heath Lane.

My comment when I saw it, was that its glass fibre body resembled an egg on wheels – a description which I don't think Geoff and Trent were very keen on. However, some time later I learned that somehow or other they had managed to turn the car over and that the body had shattered just like

THE NO HOPER

an egg . Trent said they were left sitting in the road surrounded by pieces of glass fibre not much bigger than egg shells.

Geoff gets a mention elsewhere in this book, in the chapter devoted to former students who did well in later life. I'm pretty sure Trent should be there too, but sometime after the kit car incident I lost track of him and have no idea where he went or what use he put his technology skills to.

THE CLASSICS

Despite its shortcomings in many respects, a Knutsford College education was strong on classics.

We did a lot of Shakespeare, reading the plays in class with individual students taking the parts of the various characters. The Merchant of Venice, Twelfth Night, the Tempest, MacBeth...we did them all. This meant boys had to read the female parts and this offered plenty of opportunities for humour.

I had to read the part of Lady MacBeth on one occasion and the class collapsed with laughter when I performed her soliloquy which contained the line: "Come to my woman's breasts, and take my milk for gall."

There was also considerable laughter when champion belcher Neville Kaye was selected to read the part of Sir Toby Belch in Twelfth Night.

We all had to learn passages from Shakespeare and various poems and, as a result I have found myself comparatively well read compared with friends who attended "normal" schools. Whether or not this has aided me in later life, writing stories about vicars running off with choirmaster's daughters, for the Sunday papers, I am not sure.

But it wasn't all Shakespeare and Dickens and Co. We did more up-to-date classics by authors such as H.G. Wells and A.G. Macdonald, whose "England their England" sticks in my mind because it contains a hilarious description of a village cricket match. Well, it would, wouldn't it?

Poems we did included Horatious at the Bridge, by Thomas Babington Macauley – a particular favourite of mine – and If, by Rudyard Kipling

All this exposure to art and literature clearly influenced the impressionable young minds of Percy Hope's students, many of who began to produce works which they claimed as their own but which were of a somewhat less classical nature.

THE NO HOPER

One such was:
"Down in the lavatory, dark and deep,
Two little turds lay fast asleep.
Do not disturb them, let them rest,
For Beecham's Pills have done their best."

Malcolm Goostrey's family ran the village bakery at Mobberley in those days and he had to endure hearing the following masterpiece put together by a classmate:

"Eat Goostrey's bread and shit like lead,
Fart like thunder, no bloody wonder."

Another "poem" learned off by heart by many students started:

"T'was on the good ship Venus,
By hell you should have seen us.
The figure head was a whore in bed
And the foremast was a penis."

There were a lot of farmers' sons at the college and they all seemed to claim to have composed the following:

"If a fella met a fella in a field of fitches,
Could a fella tell a fella where a fella itches?

The listener would then be asked how many f's were in that and after working out there were nine would be told that there were no f's in the word that!

I've since learned that the rhyme is well known and almost certainly did not originate from Knutsford College. What a fitch is exactly is a more difficult one. According to some it is a polecat while others say it is the

THE NO HOPER

flowering herb fennel. The worrying thing is that all these years later, I can still remember these silly rhymes but am still a duffer when it comes to mathematics!

Still, the award for the longest memory must go to the student who was said to be able to recite Eskimo Nell from beginning to end.

Eskimo who?

A SPORTING LIFE

Over the years, Knutsford College had a good reputation for sport – at least for football and cricket. For most of my time there these were the only sports played on a regular basis – apart from the annual sports day, of course, which was held on a Saturday and was attended by a fair number of parents and other family members.

Every week, students had a full afternoon devoted to either football or cricket, depending on the time of year. Teams would be picked representing the school's two houses, Nelson and Marlborough. Sometimes they would be picked to try and ensure teams of equal strength in the hope of a closely fought game.

I was not really keen on football – not being very good at it. I have already described how Bob Jackson and I would sneak off to Booth's Lake to sail model yachts to escape playing football. Nobody seemed to miss us and I suppose that sums up our respective abilities.

But when the school team hosted a side from another Cheshire school and the opportunity arose for an afternoon off to cheer on our team, we and just about every other boy suddenly became football fans. We didn't always get our way,

A college soccer team from before my time

of course, and I can remember many times having to sit through lessons, hearing the noise of football faintly in the distance.

We would get to hear the result of the game later and my recollection is that we usually won. But the actual score and details of scorers, great saves, etc. only reached us via the rumour mill.

One day I hit on an idea to change things. It was during David Wrigley's period at the school and he was the master in charge of organising the game. I suggested to him I should be allowed to attend the match as a reporter, that I should write a report and pin it up on the notice board in the passageway near the cloakroom. That way, the whole school would get to know how the team had fared.

Rather to my surprise he liked the idea and I was appointed the official match reporter – possibly on the strength of my proven writing ability or perhaps because I let it be known my father was a former sports editor of the Liverpool Evening Express. I made myself a cardboard "Press" badge and prepared for the big day.

However, word soon got around about my little ruse and a number of other boys approached Mr Wrigley and suggested that it would be impossible for one person to cover the match adequately and I would need an assistant. So when the match started there were about half-a-dozen boys sporting cardboard "Press" badges on the touchline – so many in fact that permission was given for the whole school to watch the match.

I duly wrote my report unaided by any of my assistants, typed it up on my Dad's typewriter that night and pinned it up on the notice board the following morning. Later in the day, I spotted Jimmy reading it and, on seeing me, he turned and said: "That's a good report, Skentelbery. I enjoyed reading it."

Needless to say, Knutsford College had won the game and I had heaped praise on every member of the team.

Whether or not this experience aided me at all in my future career, I don't know. But it might be worth mentioning here that many years later, when reporting a "proper" football match for a regional evening newspaper, I had a mental block, forgot that the teams had changed ends at half time

THE NO HOPER

and awarded a goal to the wrong team! Fortunately, another reporter sitting next to me in the press box, heard me dictating my report over the telephone and kindly corrected me before the error got into print.

Knutsford College had two excellent goalkeepers during my time there. A boy named Jones and Barrie Taylor. And then they had me. Yes, I did play for the school once – as goalkeeper.

Jones was there during my early days and I remember him as a calm, unflappable player who seemed to have the ability to be in the right place at the right time and so managed to make saving superb shots look easy. Taylor came later and struck me as a brash, confident youngster who was nearly always in the wrong place at the wrong time but still managed to make superb, diving saves. He impressed me greatly – probably because he was everything that I wasn't.

I remember playing as a fullback once, during one of our weekly games periods, with Barrie Taylor in goal. For once, his wanderings had left him hopelessly stranded outside the goal area with the ball trickling slowly towards the goal line and him powerless to do anything about it. I, on the other hand, was probably near enough to have run across and cleared the ball by kicking it wide of the goal. But to be on the safe side I ran across and stopped it with my hand.

Today, I am told, my action would be considered most unsporting but Denis Leighton was refereeing, congratulated me on my quick thinking and awarded a penalty.

"There is always a chance it will be saved," he explained.

The penalty was taken and Barrie saved it without batting an eyelid

"I knew you would save it," I said. And I probably did.

Some time later, Barrie left Knutsford College. But he returned to look up old friends one day and, as it was games day, he was allowed to play – in goal, of course.

As he was no longer a pupil he could flout the rules openly and kept goal with a cigarette dangling from his mouth. But when a shot came in, he happened to have his cigarette in his left hand. He dived to his right,

THE NO HOPER

collected the flying ball under his right arm, crashed to the ground in what I can only describe as a belly flop and managed to hang on to both the ball and the cigarette.

He appeared to have lost none of his skills.

But wait, I hear you say. It's no good going on about Jones and Taylor. A few paragraphs back you said you too had played for the school in goal - once. What happened in that match?

OK – I admit it. I was hoping the reader would have forgotten that careless slip.

I don't know how I ever came to be selected for the school football team. It must have been because I had started playing in goal in the weekly games lessons because it seemed less arduous than any other position. Or perhaps it was just because I was a big lad and occupied more of the goalmouth than any other boy available. And it is true that at this moment in history Knutsford College was no longer strong at football, or any other sport.

The match was against Whitehouse School at Northwich. We lost 8-0 – but in my defence I must say that if it hadn't been for me, it would have been 9-0. The one I saved came from the boot of a boy named David Hatton, who had previously been a student at Knutsford but had transferred to Whitehouse.

As I dived and pushed the ball wide of the goal, he said "Great save" but I suspect this was to excuse his own failure rather than to praise my success. My response was: "Thanks – but it's a bit late now!"

I was, of course, the official reporter for the match as well as the goalkeeper. I waxed lyrical about how the overworked defence had struggled heroically but had been let down by our forwards.

I mean to say – when a team loses 8-0 it can't just be the goalie's fault. Er...can it?

Jimmy's interest in my football reports encouraged me to publish a school magazine, "The Woodsider", which was also pinned on the notice board. I wrote much of it myself but managed to persuade a number of other boys to contribute. But such was the lack of interest among my fellow students that I never attempted to produce another.

THE SUMMER GAME

I have many clear memories of cricket at Knutsford College. Well, I would, wouldn't I?

The weekly games periods in the summer provided plenty of opportunity for inter-house matches. In my early days there were plenty of good players and the matches were keenly contested. But as the years past and the number of pupils began to fall so did the quality of the opposition. It eventually reached the stage where I was the only half-decent player left. I'm not boasting here – I really did not have much competition.

There were about three or four boys who stood out from the rest – I recall Joe Ashley, Gary Lewis, Brian Brighouse and, I think, Roger Patchett. The only way to achieve two reasonably balanced teams was to put me on one and the other four on the other. Both sides were then made up with what was left.

Joe was actually an excellent wicket keeper and, having a good eye for a ball, a natural batsman who, never having received anything in the way of coaching, could hit the ball hard and high but needed a bit of luck on his side. Gary was a reasonable slow bowler, Brian could bowl slow medium and Roger wasn't a bad wicket keeper. But nobody else had any idea.

It was in these circumstances that I managed to achieve the remarkable bowling figures of 14 wickets for no runs in one match when I was captaining one of the teams.

Demon bowler

In later years, when playing for various cricket clubs, I have been greeted with disbelief when I have recounted this tale. I mean – it could not really have happened could it? Well, it did. My success was based on sheer

THE NO HOPER

pace. I simply terrified the rookie batsmen forced to face me. And I managed to take 14 wickets when there were only 11 players in the team

because they were bowled out for such a low score that we made them bat again.

Some time after my 14th wicket, one terrified youth stuck his bat out and managed to top-edge the ball over the wicket keeper's head for four runs.

I was so disgusted I took myself off.

Another of these weekly games sticks in my memory for one amusing incident.

Somebody hit the ball hard and high – virtually straight up. The ball went up and up until it became a tiny dot against the sky. Numerous fielders gathered beneath, hands held ready to take the catch, but still the ball climbed higher.

Then farmer's son Frank Dakin, a big lad, who had been fielding some distance away, decided to join the crowd.

Actually, Frank wasn't big – he was massive. Tall, broad, muscular, powerful. A veritable man-mountain who had acquired the nickname "Bomber" – pronounced "Bomba".

He ran towards the spot where everyone expected the ball to fall, his eyes fixed firmly on the tiny dot in the sky which was now beginning its inevitable descent to earth, gaining speed as it fell.

Frank, and everyone else, was looking up, trying to judge exactly where the ball would eventually fall. He realised that as a latecomer, he might not reach the spot and accelerated, ploughing into his teammates, scattering them like skittles.

He judged his run accurately and ended up, standing like a colossus with his eyes on the ball, hands cupped above his head, precisely where the ball finally fell and completely unaware of the fallen bodies around his feet.

Yes, you've guessed it. He dropped it.

How the other team howled!

THE NO HOPER

I have already described the occasion when I first played for the school team – the evening match against Cross Town School when we bowled them out for three.

It was some years before we played another inter-school match and that was against Belmont College, away from home.

Neville Kaye skippered our team – and rightly so. He was a fine cricketer – a technically correct but aggressive batsman and a very fast bowler.

Doug Griffiths has confessed that he wasn't keen on cricket and that the main reason for this was a fear of Neville Kaye's bowling. Neville would only be half-way through his lengthy run when Doug would be on his way off the field, anxious to spend the rest of the match watching from the comparative safety of the boundary.

Neville was indeed a fast bowler but I wasn't frightened of him because by this time he and I were both members of Knutsford Cricket Club and spent most of our spare time practising in the nets at the Mere Heath Lane ground. Often we had the place to ourselves and would take it in turns, batting and bowling. So I was well used to facing his lively bowling and often went home bruised and battered.

On Saturdays we would both quite regularly play for Knutsford 2nd XI and although I can't remember much about those games I suspect Neville did rather better than I did. The only game I can remember is one when only five members of our team had arrived when play was due to start and the captain instructed me to go in and stay there until the rest of the team had arrived.

I remembered the advice of my coach, Jack Tipping, and defended stoutly with a straight bat. I batted for 75 minutes, scoring only seven runs, by which time our missing players had mostly arrived.

When I was finally dismissed I was congratulated by my captain on carrying out his wishes. I confidently expected to be headline news in the Knutsford Guardian the following week and was mortified when my heroics did not even get a mention.

THE NO HOPER

But to return to the school game at Belmont College. John White and I opened the batting and put on a good score. John dominated the partnership, scoring some 30 or 40 while I again applied the Jack Tipping theory and accumulated a patient 12. At least I thought I did. I always used to count my runs as I scored them and was quite pleased with my performance as I walked off the field only to look in the scorebook and see I had only been credited with nine!

Neville then went in and plundered some quick runs to ensure we set our opponents a good target.

He then struck sheer terror into the hearts of the Belmont batsmen and with the help of other bowlers – possibly including me – bowled them out cheaply to win the match. It was probably the last cricket match Knutsford College ever won.

The following day, Jimmy approached me and, somewhat to my surprise, said he had heard I had played well and asked how many I had scored.

"Well, Sir," I replied. "I think I got 12 but according to Himsworth (Peter Himsworth, who had kept score) I only got nine."

Jimmy nevertheless congratulated me – but I never got over those three missing runs. I bet they were put against John White's name in the scorebook.

It was quite some time before the school team played again. But when it did it could be described as a Test series. We played three matches against an Old Boys team over a period of several weeks at Knutsford Cricket Club's ground.

I'm not sure how these matches came to be organised but it may have had something to do with Neville Kaye who had recently left school and thus qualified for the Old Boys' team. In fact, the Old Boys XI consisted largely of Knutsford 2nd XI players. Apart from Neville I recall Horace Townsend, Ken Andrew, Derek Andrew, Russell Kaye and Gerry Osmond, all of who had attended the school in earlier years.

The school team was not as strong as it had been. I was appointed captain, mainly because of my continued membership of the cricket club and

THE NO HOPER

knowledge of the ground. Charlie Pemberton was a good player – he was by now a member of Timperley Cricket Club – and Geoff Aldridge was an excellent wicket keeper and useful left-hand batsman. But I don't recall anyone else who stood out.

We lost two of the three games but managed to draw the middle one. In the first, Charlie and I – who always had a friendly rivalry going on between us – both batted well against the superior bowling of the club players.

Charlie was out first and when I followed him soon after and went into the changing room he enquired: "How many did you get?"

I replied: "14"

"Drat it," he replied, with a grin. "I got 14 too – I was hoping you'd only got 13." That was Charlie and I.

No-one else got many and the Old Boys won easily.

The second game is the one I remember best – partly because we didn't lose, partly because I did better than Charlie but mostly because my Mum and Dad came to watch. The only time they ever did.

Although they followed my cricketing career with interest, they did it from afar. My Dad played with me in the garden and on Knutsford Heath and he did take me to join Knutsford Cricket Club as a junior. He even took his lawn mower onto Knutsford Heath to cut a wicket for us. But he was nearly always working on a Saturday so I suppose it's fair to say he didn't have much opportunity.

Anyway, on this occasion they turned up. Late, of course, because my Dad didn't get home from the office until gone 6pm, would need to have his dinner and it was a good walk from Stanley Road to Mere Heath Lane.

The match had started before I noticed them – sitting on a bench near the entrance to the ground. Shy Dad would not have wanted to go up to the pavilion where there was a crowd of people – Jimmy, other teachers, members of the club and, of course, a crowd of fellow students – mostly boarders let loose for the evening.

THE NO HOPER

Fortunately Jimmy spotted them and sent one of the boys to invite them to join the crowd and they did. I think he even bought them a drink.

I don't remember bowling in any of the three games against the Old Boys. I can't believe that I didn't because I was probably by now the best bowler in the school.

But as captain, I probably had some strange notion that I might appear pushy if I put myself on to bowl. I still had some of my Dad's shyness.

But as the Old Boys batted, I did take two catches – one of them to dismiss my old pal Neville Kaye.

I remember it particularly because I didn't think he was out. He hit the ball straight to me and I caught it – but I was pretty sure it was a bump-ball. For the uninitiated that means it was trapped between the end of his bat and the ground and bounced up before reaching me.

Someone fielding some distance from the wicket appealed and Denis Leighton, who was umpiring, gave Neville out.

"But, sir," said I. "It was a bump ball."

"Out!" repeated Denis – and Neville walked off the field.

I went to Geoff Aldridge, who was keeping wicket, and asked him: "Did you think that was out?"

"Oh yes, definitely!"

Several other fielders agreed with him.

Later, when I got a chance to talk to Neville, I apologised.

"I know it was a bump ball," I said.

"Don't worry about it," he replied. "The umpire is always right."

I suppose that is an indication that Knutsford College turned out boys with the right sporting spirit. Not all schools do that these days.

After the match, incidentally, several of the Old Boys who were also Knutsford 2nd XI players came to me and said: "You would have dropped both those catches if you had been playing for us."

I knew they were probably right – my shyness would have even affected my fielding when playing with "grown-ups".

THE NO HOPER

When we batted, Charlie Pemberton and I again provided the main resistance. I'm not sure how many Charlie got but he was out before me and I think he got 12. Deprived of my main partner I fell back on the advice of Jack Tipping and applied the straight back to nearly every ball, content to simply try and score a single on the last ball of each over to try and ensure a succession of rookie partners did not have to face too much bowling.

I was eventually out for 25 but had lasted long enough for the match to end in a draw.

Three things happened afterwards that stick in my mind. Charlie shook my hand, congratulated me and acknowledged that on the day I was "the better man." Praise indeed!

Then Jimmy bought me a shandy. And finally my Mum told me she had heard other boys saying that "as long as 'Skent' stays in we've got a chance." At long last I had acquired a respectable nickname.

After this, the third match was something of an anti-climax. The Old Boys must have been struggling to raise a team because they had quite a few players who were not former students, including one Don Bailey who went on to captain nearby Toft Cricket Club the year they won the national village cricket club tournament, the final of which was played on Lancashire's Old Trafford ground.

Again, Charlie Pemberton and I found ourselves batting together and when he was out I heard one of the opposition fielders say "now we've only got to get rid of the other bugger."

I again adopted a defensive approach until the wicket keeper said to me: "I don't know why you are playing like this. You won't win if you don't go for the runs."

I allowed myself to be persuaded and hit the next ball high and handsome. It dropped just short of the boundary and my partner and I managed to run only two

"There you are," said the talkative wicket keeper. "See what you can do when you have a go."

THE NO HOPER

"I only got two," I replied.

"But it was nearly a six – next time you might be lucky."

For once ignoring the advice of Jack Tipping. I took an almighty swipe at the next delivery – and was clean bowled.

"Oh dear," said my wicket keeper friend. "You picked the wrong one."

I had got 12 – still the top score of the innings – but I could have kicked myself for in effect being "talked out".

My only consolation was that it was the demon bowler Don Bailey who got me.

The incident also made me realise something that had never occurred to me before. While I and the rest of my team took those three matches very seriously, Jimmy and the Old Boys were more interested in the piss-up afterwards.

Knutsford College only played one more cricket match and by this time the dwindling number of pupils had weakened our team considerably. Charlie Pemberton had left school and the only batting support I could expect came from farmer's son Joe Ashley, a natural hitter with a good eye for the ball who, on his day and with a good deal of luck, could hit the ball far and wide.

But he fell off a hay wagon and broke his arm a few days before the match.

Our opponents were Whitehouse School from the Northwich area and the game was played on Lostock Gralam Cricket Club's ground.

I have to admit that on that occasion I was a thoroughly objectionable character. I don't know what had got into me. I can only assume that I had decided that a display of confidence would improve our chances.

In fact, I was far from confident. The night before I had sought my father's advice about what to do if I won the toss.

"I would always bat first," he said.

So when the coin came down in my favour I sneered and confidently said: "We'll bat." When the opposing captain gave a huge sigh of relief I immediately realised I had made a big mistake.

THE NO HOPER

There was a strong wind blowing when I sent my two opening batsmen out.
What's that? You want to know why I wasn't one of the openers myself? Well I always liked to see what the bowling was like before I went in. Cowardly, I know, but if Don Bradman could do it, why not I?
I didn't get much of a look at the bowling. The White House opening bowler was a tall, strong lad who took a 20-yard run and hurled the ball down at a frightening pace. Apparently he played for Lostock Gralam so he was on his home ground. I think he took three balls to dismiss our opening batsman – which left me with three balls of the first over to face.
He was bowling into the wind which meant the ball swung prolifically in the air so I had little option but to fall back on Jack Tipping's advice again. I survived the over and, in fact got a run when the ball hit the edge of my bat and hurtled through the slip fielders.
This took me to the other end to face the other opening bowler who was also good, although not as good as the big lad. I could cope with him and managed to get a few runs over the next few overs.
However my team mates could not handle the big lad and wickets fell rapidly. I was having trouble with him too and most of my runs at that end came off the edge of the bat.
Eventually the lesser bowler sent down a really bad ball to me. So bad that the Whitehouse teacher who was umpiring and must have been feeling sorry for us, shouted "Hit it!"
I had already decided to do just that and hit it for four. Not content with that, I insolently told the umpire: "I don't need telling when to hit it."
He must have thought me a cheeky young pup – and he would have been right.
It could have had something to do with him giving me out LBW later on. But I could be doing him a disservice – he may not have known that the laws of cricket state that a batsman cannot be out LBW if the ball pitches outside the line of the leg stump.

THE NO HOPER

Anyway, we were all out for 30. I got 15 of them and Gary Lewis was the next highest scorer with two.

That didn't give us much of a chance but I still tried to put on a brave face. I was considered a fast bowler by my teammates but I knew I was not in the same class as the big Whitehouse lad. I decided if I tried to bowl into the wind, as he had, I would be reduced to a very pedestrian pace. I would bowl with the wind behind me.

It turned out the two opening batsmen were the same pair who had opened their bowling – in fact I don't think they used any other bowlers. The big lad took first strike.

I decided to disguise the fact that I was going to bowl fast by taking a very short run – just ambling up to the stumps like a slow bowler but then using my back to generate pace. It worked perfectly. The delivery was fast, aided by the wind, and straight and true. It clean bowled him.

I don't know who was most surprised, the batsman, me or the rest of my team.

"That'll do nicely," I said calmly.

My next couple of thunderbolts did not fool the new batsman so I decided to slip in a slow one to try and deceive him. But it didn't – he hit it for a single which brought the other opening batsman down to face the last ball of my over.

I decided to try the same trick again – a fast ball delivered from a slow, ambling run. It worked – I clean bowled him too.

Two wickets for one run in the first over. Perhaps we still stood a chance.

Alas, no. I could not take another wicket and their third and fourth batsmen had no problem with our other bowlers.

So we lost – and to rub salt in the wound the match was reported in the Knutsford Guardian!

Other sports

Apart from football and cricket, the only other sports played at the college during my time there were tennis and table tennis.
Tennis was played one summer only - although I understand it had been played regularly in earlier years.
A grass court was prepared on the lawn and we students organised a tournament among ourselves.
Odds on favourite to win was Joe Ashley, because of his cannonball service. But Gary Lewis was also considered a likely champion.
In the event, Lewis was knocked out by Bob Jackson, largely on account of Bob's repeated use of the drop-shot. Well, I'll call it a drop shot – really he couldn't hit the ball hard enough to reach his opponent!
I played Joe Ashley in the final and took the first set narrowly.
The bell then went for the end of the mid-day break so the match was suspended, to be finished later.
But it never was - so I hereby claim the title. I doubt if it will be challenged now...although knowing Joe...!
Table tennis had a much longer existence at the school, although students from earlier times will doubtless be surprised to know it was ever played.
What happened was that Jimmy displayed his joinery skills to make us a table tennis table. It was made of hardboard on a timber frame and was slightly smaller than a full-size table tennis table. There were a number of nail-heads, of course, and if the ball struck one these it would have a much higher bounce and could veer off in any direction.
There must have only been three classes at the school by now because the table was placed in the old 2B classroom.
That was where I learned my table tennis, although some of the others, Charlie Pemberton and Geoff Aldridge included, had obviously played previously.
I had no forehand shots and this put me at a great disadvantage when playing Charlie. Such was the keen rivalry between us in all matters

THE NO HOPER

sporting that I remember going home one night when my parents were out and spending a whole evening practising forehand shots on the dining table pushed up against a wall.

After that I had a forehand and could give Charlie a game, but I fancy he always had the better of me.

I started to play regularly at the youth club at Brook Street Chapel in Knutsford and eventually arranged a match between the club and the college - played on the club's full size table. Our team consisted of Charlie, Geoff, myself and someone else whose name escapes me.

Despite having to adapt our play for what, to us, was an unfamiliar table, we won.

A return match was played at the college one winter evening which we won easily on Jimmy's hardboard table.

To our surprise, Jimmy laid on tea and biscuits for both teams.

Boxing was not a sport encouraged at Knutsford College, at least during my time there. In earlier days I believe it was. Doug Griffiths says the boarders had boxing sessions of an evening and he recalls being frequently "knocked down" by John White.

But fights occasionally took place, usually on the cricket field which was screened from the school building by trees and the infamous holly bushes which I had encountered on my second day at the school.

These fights were not widely publicised but usually attracted a large number of spectators. In fact, let's be honest, they were not spectators but more of a baying mob.

Somehow or other I got involved in one of these fights during my embarrassing first term. I had not, as far as I was aware, made any enemies so someone must have simply decided it would make good entertainment to match me up with some other boy in a fight. For some reason, they selected tough, farmer's son Mark Ashley as my opponent.

We barely knew one another and certainly had not quarrelled. But that was irrelevant. The fight had to take place.

THE NO HOPER

The main difference between Mark and I was that he was quite prepared to throw heavy punches at me while I was not willing to return them. Mercifully he aimed most of his blows at my arms, but they still hurt. I merely attempted, not very successfully, to dodge and parry his blows.

The crowd soon got fed up with such a boring contest so it was decided that instead of Mark I should face his younger brother Joe – who has already been mentioned in this chronicle for his tennis and his failure to help the school cricket team due to breaking his arm at an inconvenient time.

Joe and I were actually good friends but I think he was chosen as he was quite small – certainly much smaller than me – and it was thought that the spectacle of a big lad being thrashed by a little 'un would be more amusing.

In fact, if that was the idea, it did not work. We simply circled each other without seriously trying to land any blows and the spectators soon became bored

Most of the fights that took place on the cricket field paid little regard to Marquis of Queensbury Rules but I recall one that did – well, in a manner of speaking. It took place between John Stringer and John Westwood – two completely different boys.

Stringer was a dour, stocky character, probably a bit below average height who had earned himself the nickname "Bulldog." Westwood was taller, of sallow complexion and much slimmer build. For some reason he was known as "Isaac."

What their dispute was about I have no idea but I think it must have been considered serious one judging by the lengths they went to organise a proper bout.

Westwood's parents owned a sports shop in Altrincham and on the day of the fight, he brought two pairs of boxing gloves, presumably from the shop.

When the fight started it soon became apparent that Westwood had boxed before and that Stringer had not. As a result, Westwood was able to land a

THE NO HOPER

series of blows which clearly stung his opponent, although the pain inflicted was probably not so much physical but more to his pride.

The usual baying mob soon gathered and the fight seemed to go on for a long time with the noise level climbing higher and higher.

Eventually Westwood landed a blow to Stringer's face with started his nose bleeding – and caused him to lose his temper. He launched a series of wild, uncontrolled pile-drivers which, if they had found their target would probably have ended the fight with Westwood unconscious on the ground.

But the nimble Isaac evaded them all and was able to land a few more well-aimed blows which enraged Bulldog even more.

Just how the fight ended I don't know. It just seemed to peter out. Perhaps someone spotted authority approaching in the form of one of the teachers or perhaps Stringer finally capitulated. But I am pretty sure that Westwood was judged the winner by common consent.

Neither contestant was a particular friend of mine, but years later when I was a reporter on the Knutsford Guardian, I was covering the magistrates' court one day when Stringer appeared for a minor motor cycling offence. I don't know if he spotted me sitting at the press bench or, if he did, he guessed why the case was not reported in the paper. My sense of loyalty to a former colleague at the college caused me to have a convenient loss of memory on the way back to the office. It was, after all, a trivial offence which today would not find its way into any newspaper.

I should say here, however, that if he had recognised me in court and had asked me not to report the case, I would have been torn between two loyalties because reporters were not expected to accede to such requests.

CRIME AND PUNISHMENT

It might be convenient here to insert a few words on the summary punishment handed out at Knutsford College when some offence was committed and some pupil who, on the balance of probabilities, was identified as the likely offender.

I have already referred to an incident when I was grabbed by the collar and shaken by Jimmy in circumstances which I considered were a touch unfair. I have also described the painful knuckle-rapping administered by Mr Dawson for offences as minor as yawning in class.

Many fellow students have told me of being caned by Percy, sometimes in front of the whole school. One claimed our headmaster had beaten him so hard that the cane snapped. He seemed quite proud of this.

There are also stories of boys who slipped an exercise book down their trousers before being caned – and got away with it. Knowing Percy, I find this hard to believe as I am sure he would have detected such a ruse.

The Hall - where canings usually took place

I have mentioned previously that Percy was a keen horse rider and usually had several horses stabled around the building. As such, he possessed a riding crop.

Need I say more? Well, I will, anyway.

In a wooded area roughly between the football field and the cricket field there was a summer house which I am sure was officially out-of-bounds. But whether or not, it frequently played a central role in various games. Fort, Indian camp, castle. It could be anything.

But on one occasion it was the scene of what was considered a most serious offence when news of it reached Percy.

THE NO HOPER

Two boys were grabbed by a group of older students, dragged into the summer house and debagged. It was probably seen as a huge joke by the perpetrators, but the two victims were clearly seriously shocked and distressed. So much so that they did the unthinkable - they reported the matter to a teacher.

Percy was outraged when he heard of it. The culprits – I think there were about four of them - were brought before the whole school at assembly and beaten with the riding crop without, as far as I know, any opportunity to plead their innocence or guilt.

They received six strokes each and although they each did their best to take the punishment without showing any sign of pain, I vividly remember one struggling to hold back tears and sobbing as he limped out of the room after the sixth stroke.

It was quite unusual for beatings like this to take place in front of the whole school. Usually they were administered in the hall outside. It was, I suppose, an indication of how serious Percy considered the offence. I don't think there any further similar incidents in the summer house or anywhere else, after that.

SHAME

I would hope that by now, the reader will have noted that I have not shied away from describing incidents which at the time were a source of embarrassment to me and which in some cases remain so today. I have also admitted being an obnoxious youth on the day of the last cricket match the college ever played.

But there was one incident about which I have always felt deep shame – even though it was not really my fault.

Peter Webb was a quiet, mild-mannered boy of around my age who I suspect had suffered a similarly difficult introduction to life at Knutsford College to the one I had experienced.

I don't know this for certain. He was not a close friend of mine and I spent little time in his company. He had his own group of close friends and and I think they all travelled to school together by train from somewhere in the Northwich area. So I could be wrong. He certainly seemed to accept his nickname – "Spider" - rather more readily than I had accepted Skentelbollocks.

But to be quiet and mild-mannered was not a recipe to be accepted as "one of the gang" and Peter had the additional misfortune to be the possessor of a pair of rather large, protruding ears. This made him a target for ridicule by some of the less sensitive members of the school community.

He frequently fell victim to pranksters who would creep up behind him and finger-flick his ears – which, as anyone who has suffered this treatment knows, can be quite painful on a cold, frosty morning.

Before anyone gets the wrong idea, I was not a party to any of this. The early traumas I had suffered on arrival at Knutsford College had made me realise the effect this could have and I think over the years I had a good track record in trying to help timid youngsters if or when I became aware of their plight.

No, the shame I still feel today, stems from something else.

THE NO HOPER

During one school holiday, Peter Webb died of leukaemia. Because it was a holiday time, I knew nothing about it – and indeed still knew nothing about it until the start of the new term when Peter wasn't there any more.

But apparently it was decided it would be a fitting gesture if six of his classmates acted as pall bearers at his funeral.

I was out somewhere when Percy telephoned and asked my mother if I would be one of the six.

My mother, it seems, still thought of me as being someone who needed protection from the harsh realities of life.

She didn't exactly refuse his request but said something on the lines of "Oh, I don't know – he's never even been to a funeral."

Percy lost his cool a bit – and I don't blame him – and snapped: "Well he'll have to go to one some day."

How the conversation ended I don't know. It was months later before I found out about it.

But I have always felt a sense of shame that I was not considered grown-up enough to have performed that simple task for a classmate.

Percy was right, of course. I did have to attend many funerals – the first of which was his.

WHAT'S IN A NAME

I have a middle name – George. It's not a name I particularly like or dislike. I am not proud of it, nor am I ashamed of it. It is not a name I own nor disown. It is simply there.

But I was utterly baffled when, on discovering it, a significant number of my school mates thought it a huge joke. The hilarity it provoked brought back memories of the laughter which my unusual surname had provoked on my first day at the school. It was almost like "Skentelbollocks" all over again.

It still makes no sense to me. I mean, for God's sake, we've had six kings named George so the name should command some respect, even if one of them was apparently mad!

Anyway, once the laughter finally subsided, it resulted in me becoming known as George throughout the school for a period. I'm not sure how long it lasted, but it must have been around the time of that infamous 8-0 football defeat because I clearly remember hearing the phrase "George played badly" as we waited miserably for the train back home after the match.

Denis Leighton had accompanied us on that trip and sprang to my defence. I heard him respond: "George did NOT play badly." I was pleased to hear him say it – but even the bloody teachers were calling me George!

Looking back on it, in committing that disastrous match to posterity in this book, I could have blamed a fictitious brother for the debacle. But I guess it's a little late for that.

During the time when I was known as George, a group of first formers, led by Geoff Aldridge and Barry Grosvenor, spent the greater part of a maths lesson (presumably after Jimmy had left for his daily trip to the Legh Arms) on researching what classmates' names would be if spelled backwards.

THE NO HOPER

Thus George Skentelbery became "Egroeg Yrebletneks" – but pronounced by the originators of this highly intellectual pastime as "Eegrog Reblitinicks."

I hit back with "Foeg Eggdirdler" and "Yrrab Ronevsorg" – names which I later used for aliens in a science fiction story I was writing at the time.

My name-change resulted in one other amusing incident. A school pal called at my home during the summer holidays and asked my mother: "Is George in?"

She sent him next door where, coincidentally, a "real" George lived.

Even she did not think of me as George, even though I had been given my middle name in memory of her brother – the uncle I never knew - who had died tragically from cancer at the age of 30.

He had been a great cricketer and I inherited the bat he had been awarded for scoring a century in the last match he played in prior to his death. I used that bat during most of my time at Knutsford College and for a good part of my club cricket career as well. I still have it today. You would expect me to mention that, I am sure.

Although I never used the name George, I liked to use the initials "DG" when my name was entered in a cricket scorebook. They were, of course, the same initials as the great Australian cricketer Don Bradman and in my foolish youthfulness I thought perhaps they might result in some of his greatness being passed on to me.

Well, I would, wouldn't I?"

AN INSPECTOR CALLS

I'm pretty sure that it was during the last term, shortly before Jimmy finally announced the closure of Knutsford College, that we had a visit from a school inspector. Whether there was a connection between these two events, I cannot say.

But it's fair to say we students did little to enhance the school's reputation during the visit. The inspector was a woman – which might seem strange at a boys' school - but there we are.

The lady came, she saw and she departed and it was not too long afterwards that we learned about the impending closure.

It was the only time during my time at the college that we had an inspection and whether any were carried out previously I do not know.

The first school inspectors in England were appointed in 1837 to monitor the effectiveness of government grants to Church of England and non-denominational elementary schools. Ten years later, the inspection programme was expanded to include Roman Catholic schools. It was not until 1902 that inspection of state-funded secondary schools started, with the inspections carried out by local authority inspectors.

Today, there is an Independent Schools Inspectorate which, monitored by Ofsted – the Office for Standards in Education, – inspects schools which are members of the Independent Schools Council (ISC). Independent schools which are not members of ISC are inspected by Ofsted, which of course inspects all state schools and was set up in 1992. But who inspected private schools in the 1940s and 1950s I do not know and given that no prior inspections were carried out during my time at the college it seems possible that both Percy and Jimmy escaped any official scrutiny.

Anyway, our lady inspector, wherever she came from, seemed reasonable enough. She sat in on some lessons and on occasions actually took a class. I recall she took a lesson during which she set us an essay to write.

THE NO HOPER

This was right up my street, particularly as the subject was "A memorable occasion", which meant we could more or less choose our own subject. I wrote about a cricket match – as you would expect, wouldn't you?

I think I chose the match in which Denis Leighton had changed the rules to allow me to hit a six off the last ball and so win the match. Well, I would, wouldn't I?

Predictably, I have to say, she singled it out for praise although I don't think she read it out to the class.

However, whatever impression she formed about the academic ability of the students of Knutsford College from her time in the classroom, I fear her report was probably influenced more by the informal chat she had with a group of us on the lawn during the mid-day break. She seemed particularly interested in extra-curricular activities. What did we do when we not at school? How did we think we compared with other similar schools? How did we perform in sports competitions against other schools?

I don't think we had played any inter-school matches since the humiliation of the 8-0 defeat at football at Belmont College and the debacle of the cricket match at Whitehouse School, so morale was pretty low. We made no secret of the fact that we thought that, as a school, we were rubbish.

Somehow she learned I was a member of Knutsford Cricket Club – and before anyone says "Well, she would, wouldn't she?" I am pretty sure it wasn't me that told her. Honest!

"Well" she said, brightly: "That's pretty good, isn't it?"

There was a silence and then Barry Grosvenor, a boarder who for some strange reason had been sent to a school in Cheshire despite the fact that he lived in the London area, said unenthusiastically: "Well, he is about the best, I suppose."

His words have remained entrenched in my memory for more than 60 years because Barry – fine fellow although he undoubtedly was - did not know one end of a cricket bat from the other.

THE NO HOPER

About the best, indeed! Our conversation with the lady inspector continued for some time, during which we could find precious little to say about our school which might persuade her to go away and write positive report.
I can only guess what she might have said and what Jimmy might have thought about it.

THE LAST TERM

Just how the news eventually leaked out that the school was to close, I can't recall. We should have seen it coming, I suppose, because for some time Jimmy had been getting rid of stuff which would clearly be of use at a school. Books, sports equipment, desks.

At assembly, one day, he asked if anyone was interested in home movies. Bob Jackson and I both had 9.5 mm film projectors at home and both put our hands up. Jimmy explained that he had a collection of films he didn't want and said we could have them if we wanted.

We practically snatched his hand off and went home with dozens of old black and white, silent films, dramas, westerns, comedies, cartoons, etc. Some starred Charlie Chaplin, some Laurel and Hardy. One, I recall, was a silent version of "Blackmail," an Alfred Hitchcock film which was quite famous as the first British "talkie." Bob and I shared them out on the kitchen table at my house.

When the news of the school closure was finally confirmed, My Dad was somewhat annoyed. I was 15 and, he believed, due to sit examinations to obtain my School Leaving Certificate, or whatever it was called in those days.

How was I to obtain documentary evidence that I had received any sort of education at all?

You will note that I say this was my father's belief. In fact, I had not heard of any of my fellow students being entered for public examinations of any sort for years.

However, I believe that in earlier years things may have been different.

As already stated, the school prospectus – undated but probably from around 1927 – made the following claim:

"Boys are prepared for the Entrance Examination of the Public Schools and for the Royal Navy. The Oxford and Cambridge Local Examinations will be taken in the ordinary school course, and Boys can be prepared for any Examination that may be required. Special attention will be given to

THE NO HOPER

Sons of Commercial Gentlemen who desire their Sons to take up Commerce."

Notwithstanding this, I strongly suspect that had the school continued for the final year of my education, there would have been no opportunity for me to sit an examination unless my father organised it himself.

While news of the school's impending closure probably caused considerable anger among parents, it has to be said there was little concern shown by students.

My own main worry was that I would no longer be able to play table tennis on Jimmy's home-made table.

There was some discussion among classmates about where they might complete their schooling. I learned from my parents that they were going to send me to Grimes' Tutorial College in Manchester – a well respected establishment that specialised in "cramming" an education into students to get them through their GCEs – General Certificate of Education.

It was reputed to be very expensive - 10 guineas a term per subject was the figure being bandied about by my classmates..

But all this was an age away – after the long summer holidays. And we still had our last term at Knutsford College to complete.

I was still more bothered about the table tennis table than anything else and decided that on the last day I would approach Jimmy and ask him if he would sell it to me.

The last few weeks seemed to fly by and nothing out of the ordinary seemed to happen. Mr Goldrick did his best to carry on providing an education of some sort. It is just possible he was unaware of the looming closure, but given the fact that it was common knowledge among the boys, I doubt it. Freddy was still there, supervising games and generally helping to keep things ticking over. Jimmy was, for the most part, his usual self. That included his daily trip to the Legh Arms during the latter part of the morning, leaving First Class to descend into a state of anarchy.

When the final day dawned, however, it was clear it was not going to be a normal day. Jimmy was in a highly emotional state and I began to have

THE NO HOPER

doubts about asking him if I could buy the table tennis table. It just would not be right to raise such a mercenary subject with him when he was in such a condition

At the final assembly – which was at mid-day - he tried to give a speech. But although he made a valiant effort, he could not control his emotions. Tears rolled down his cheeks as he spoke, between sobs, of the past history of the college, of the generations of students it had sent out into the wide world and of his sorrow that he could not continue any longer.

I found myself deeply moved as I listened to my headmaster blubbering like a child in front of the whole school. The man I had, despite all his failings, looked up to for the last six years and still feared and respected, had been reduced to a pathetic wreck.

My mind was made up. I could not possibly raise the subject of the table tennis table. I would have to return to the college, the following week, perhaps. Or I could telephone.

The assembly came to an end and we students – there didn't seem to be many of us - filed out of the room, not daring to even look at the hunched figure of Jimmy sobbing uncontrollably as he stood before his assembled students for the last time.

Where the other boys went I do not know, but somehow I found myself alone in a strangely quiet cloakroom, gathering my things together before setting off home. There wasn't a sound anywhere – not from along the corridor leading to the hall and the two main classrooms, not from the adjacent kitchen where Martha Moston and Brenda and their team would normally have been rattling pots and pans as they prepared that day's lunch. It was really quite eerie.

Then suddenly, I became aware of a sound. Shuffling feet and heavy sobbing.

I stepped out of the cloakroom and into the corridor to see Jimmy, head bowed, moving slowly towards me as if in a trance. As he reached me, he stopped, looked at me through tear-filled eyes and put his hand on my shoulder.

THE NO HOPER

For a moment we stood together, headmaster and student, next to the notice board where, in happier times, I had posted my football reports and pinned-up the one-and-only issue of "The Woodsider" school magazine and where, no doubt, countless other notices had been posted over the years, detailing the past glories of Knutsford College before my time.

In that moment I had a sudden and unexpected change of mind. I WOULD raise the subject of the table tennis table because if I didn't do it then, I never would.

"Sir..." I began, hesitantly.

He looked at me, sorrow etched across his face and apparently unable to speak.

"Sir...could I buy the table tennis table?"

In an instant his whole demeanour changed. He straightened and removed his hand from my shouldeer. His face brightened and his tears vanished as if they had never been there.

"How much, boy?" he said. "How much?"

I suggested 10 shillings and he accepted with such alacrity that I wished I had offered only five.

There followed a brief conversation in which it was agreed that I would call at the college the following week to bring the money and collect the table.

This presented me with something of a problem as the table was far too heavy for one person to carry. I solved it by persuading Bob Jackson – who you may recall had left Knutsford College some time before it closed to go to Whitehouse School – to return to Woodside and help me carry the table across town.

It was strange going back to that magnificent building. Classrooms still there. Desks still in place, but no pupils. Eerily silent. No teachers, no kitchen staff.

Deserted grounds. At first we thought there was no Jimmy either, but we eventually found him, apparently recovered from the trauma of the previous week. I handed over a ten bob note and we collected the table.

THE NO HOPER

We took it to my house where it stayed in an outhouse for a while, unused. But Bob's elder sister, Hazel, ran a hairdressing salon in King Street, Knutsford, behind which was an old, two-storey barn. With her permission, we took the table there as there was just about enough room to play a decent game.

Bob and I started our own club on the upper floor of that barn, attracting a membership of around a dozen. Only two were Old Boys – Tony Walley and Joe Ashley.

Apart from table tennis, we gave film shows using the old movies we had been given by Jimmy some time previously. We also installed a record player and sold soft drinks made from flavourings used in Bob's father's pharmaceutical manufacturing company. An early sign, perhaps of some entrepreneurial skills, although if it was I am pretty sure we did not acquire them at Knutsford College.

We had many hours of fun in that building – and one drama.

Bob, Tony Walley and I were there one winter night when a crowd of drunks arrived, demanding admission. We politely declined their request and locked ourselves in. But then things got nasty.

Access to the upper floor was, in those days, via an external flight of stone steps. The drunks came up the steps and started to kick the locked door at the top. Eventually it burst open and I found myself confronted by the leader of the pack, who stood menacingly on the threshold.

I happened to be holding a long-handled brush at the time and, instinctively, charged at him, wielding the brush like a lance. It caught him in the throat, toppling him backwards. He grabbed the head of the brush but could not stop himself from falling backwards down the steps, taking the brush with him. His cronies were queuing behind him on the narrow steps and the whole gang fell backwards, like a pack of cards and ended up in a struggling pile of legs and arms on the cobbled yard at the bottom.

It was a miracle none of them were seriously injured. Probably the fact they were drunk is what saved them. But if they escaped physical injury,

THE NO HOPER

their pride was seriously bruised – particularly that of the leader who had ended up on his back still clutching the brush.

The lock on the door was, of course, smashed, and the only way we could keep the gang out now was to throw our weight against the door.

Tempers were running high in the darkness outside and I could hear the leader threatening to "wrap the bloody brush round his bloody neck." A stalemate had been reached, with only one gang member able to push at the door from the top of the steps while two of us could push from the inside.

But we were effectively trapped in the building and we realised it would only be a matter of time before the gang realised that even if they couldn't get inside there were windows to be smashed.

Fortunately, there was an old loading bay at the rear of the building and, after a whispered debate, we hatched a plan. We decided Tony – as the smallest of the three of us – could be lowered from the loading bay into a neglected garden, sneak out through a rear gate and go for help. We switched off the lights so the gang could not see what we were doing and I carried on holding the door closed while Bob lowered Tony from the loading bay. He was then able to sneak away unnoticed and run to Bob's home for help.

Bob and I continued to hold the gang at bay and it was only a short while before Bob's Dad arrived, armed with a walking stick, and weighed into the gang from the rear.

Taken completely by surprise they fled in disarray – probably unaware in the darkness that just one man was attacking them.

Looking back on the incident, I realise that Mr Jackson showed considerable courage in coming to our rescue that night. The drunks outnumbered him – and us – and while older than us, were considerably younger than him.

Membership of our club dwindled as the boys, one by one, reached the age of 18 and were called up for National Service – two years in the armed

THE NO HOPER

forces which most of us would like to have avoided but which was compulsory.

The club finally closed when Bob was called up. I never went back there and I have no idea what happened to Jimmy's table tennis table.

The barn has subsequently been renovated and is now Knutsford Heritage Centre, run by a charity who were unaware of this brief but colourful chapter in the building's history until I told them about it.

Although those external stone steps are no longer there and the ground floor is completely different today, the upper floor where our club flourished for a couple of years, is largely the same as it was then.

THE NO HOPER

THE CURRANT BUN

You had to have a good sense of humour to survive at Knutsford College. The place was full of practical jokers and if you didn't keep your wits about you the chances were you would fall victim to one of their japes.

In time you acquired some practical joking skills yourself and I must admit I became quite proficient in this respect. But the best and funniest joke I pulled off didn't come to me until after I had left school – which, of course, also means after the school had closed.

It involved a former school pal but I'm afraid he has to remain anonymous. He was furious when he discovered he had been the victim of an absolute classic and he would never forgive me if I were to reveal his identity – even after all these years. But to tell the story properly, he has to have a name so I will make one up. I'll call him Albert Entwistle, because, with due apologies to any real Albert Entwistle who happens to read this, it seems a suitable name for anyone daft enough to fall for this cruel trick.

I should mention here that Albert was one of those people who was always having things happen to him. He was older than me, but looking back on it, if there was anyone at Knutsford College who was more of a No Hoper than me, it was him. For instance, he was driving along behind a furniture van one day when the back door of the van opened and a piano rolled out and landed on his car bonnet. On another occasion he was driving along a main road and glanced out of the side window to see a car wheel and tyre bouncing along beside him.

"Look at that" he cried to his wife. "Some bloody fool has lost a wheel."

THE NO HOPER

In the next instant the rear offside corner of his car slumped, there was a horrible grinding sound and Albert discovered who the bloody fool was!

Albert left the school before it closed but I kept in touch with him over the years. Not closely, you understand, but closely enough to know when he got married, where he worked, when and where he bought his first house, when he had his first child, etc. Completely by chance, I also learned when he had a telephone installed at home.

These days when most people seem to consider ownership of the latest mobile 'phone an essential part of living, having a landline fitted at your home is pretty small beer. But in those days, the telephone service was run by the Post Office – or to give the full name, the General Post Office, or GPO. And to get a 'phone involved going on a lengthy waiting list for months, if not years.

My parents had had a 'phone at home for years and I was well used to using 'phones at the Guardian office. In fact my first job of each day was to call the police station and the fire station with a hopeful: "Anything doing?" and after that I would be making calls all day. So I was quite blasé about 'phone ownership.

But for Albert it was obviously different. It so happened that over the course of several months I bumped into him several times. On the first occasion he was in a state of great excitement because he had ordered a telephone. Next time, he was even more excited because he had been given a date, still several weeks away, when the line would be installed. Then he was positively frothing at the mouth because the handset had been delivered and he was just waiting for it to be connected. Finally, he told me he had received a letter to inform him his line would go live the following morning. He was ecstatic – full of how much his new 'phone would improve his life.

THE NO HOPER

I found the whole thing rather amusing, so much so that I went back to the office and shared the story with the staff. Chief reporter Les Groves, who knew Albert slighty, and also saw the funny side of the situation, said: "Why don't you give him a call in the morning and pretend to be a telephone engineer – you can probably have some fun with him."

It seemed a good idea – but I pointed out that Albert would probably recognise my voice. So it was agreed that Les would make the call while I listened on an extension.

Early the following morning, to ensure it was the first call to be made on the new 'phone, the following scenario was played out on Albert's 'phone.

Albert: "Hello, Knutsford 1234."

Les (putting on official sounding voice): "Mr Entwistle?"

Albert: (with obvious pride in his voice) "Yes, speaking."

Les: "GPO telephone engineers here, Mr Entwistle. Just calling to check your line is working OK.".

Albert: "Oh, yes. Thank you. It seems to be working fine."

Les: "Ah, yes, Mr Entwistle. But we must first run a few tests. Can you repeat a few phrases after me?"

Albert: "Oh yes. I think I can do that."

Les: "Right. Please repeat after me Mr Entwistle. 456893"

Albert: "456893"

THE NO HOPER

Les: "ABC THV"

Albert: "ABC THV"

Les: "Very good Mr Entwistle. Now just repeat one more phrase please. What should I do with my currant bun?"

Albert: "What should I do with my currant bun?"

Les (stifling laughter): "Stick it up your arsole!"

There followed a lengthy pause during which Les and I were rolling about, helpless with laughter.

Then an indignant Albert: "Oh, you bugger you!"

Albert lived a good 15 minute drive from the Guardian office. But that morning it took him less than 10 minutes to reach the office to play hell with us. He could not see the funny side of it – and never has done to this day.

THE AFTERMATH

The summer holiday which followed the closure in 1954 was a strange one. I wasn't sure, at first, whether I would be continuing in full-time education but eventually Dad took me into Manchester for an interview at Grimes' Tutorial College.

It was not apparent to me at the time, but Grimes' was a "cramming" institute, specifically designed to get students who, for one reason or another, had not fulfilled their parents' expectations, through their final school leaving examinations. In my case, of course, this was because my school had closed. But others needed help to gain entry to university and there was some tutorial help offered to those already at Manchester University – which was just across the road – but struggling.

I discovered that David Bate, a fellow student at Knutsford College had also been sent to Grimes' and I think we met up on the first day. A week or two later, I got a 'phone call from Joe Ashley, whose parents had somewhat belatedly decided to send him to Grimes. He cycled from his home at Plumley to mine in Knutsford to travel by train to Manchester with me for his first day. I was able to show him the ropes.

Grimes' was a very different institution to Knutsford College. For a start, there were girls. There were usually only about six students in a class – and in fact, there were only two in the art class I attended, the other being a rather attractive young lady who clearly fancied herself something rotten and looked at me as if I was something the cat had brought in.

In one class there was a Chinese girl, named Miss Wong, who wore a skirt with a long slit up the side. I was rather puzzled at the number of times my male classmates were dropping their rulers or pencils on the floor and having to bend to retrieve them but eventually I found out they were doing it deliberately so they could peer up Miss Wong's skirt.

As a well brought up former student of a school for the sons of gentlemen, I had never even thought of doing such a thing.

THE NO HOPER

I swiftly discovered my English was not as good as I had been led to believe at Knutsford. My essays did not stand out from the rest and I was frequently embarrassed by the critical comments made by my tutor.

My French improved considerably, however, partly because the subject was, for the first time in my experience, being taught properly and partly because I was rather smitten by the French mistress, despite her probably being old enough to be my mother.

One thing I needn't have worried about missing after Knutsford College closed was table tennis. The main – in fact the only - recreation provided at Grimes' was table tennis in the boys' common room in the basement. There were some excellent players there during my time and as a result of the higher standard of opposition my own play improved. I even got to the semi-finals of a tournament organised by the students themselves.

I didn't suffer the ignominy of jokes about my surname – which was quite surprising really as nicknames were commonly used. Joe Ashley was known as "Little Roundhead" and I seem to recall David Bate was sometimes referred to as "Maggot." There was a black boy who had to endure being called "Snowball" – something that would never happen today, although it didn't seem to bother him. He was a great table tennis player.

I was only taking five subjects – English Language, English Literature, Art, History and Geography. I really only took English seriously, as Dad had already told me he thought the only way forward for me was to follow him into journalism.

Some days there were lengthy periods between lessons, so there was plenty of time for table tennis. On some days I had the whole afternoon off so a group of us went skating at the old Manchester Ice Palace. Homework – something of a novelty to me after Knutsford College – was usually done on the train.

A year passed quickly and before I knew it I was taking my "O Levels" as an external candidate at Altrincham Boys' Grammar School. Strangely, I

THE NO HOPER

got quite a good pass for Art but only scraped through the two English exams.

I have always maintained the reason for a below-par performance in English language that day was the desk I was sitting at. Bear in mind, I was taking all my exams with about 30 or 40 boys who were complete strangers to me and, despite my experiences at Knutsford College, I still had a shy streak.

Another boy asked if I would mind swapping desks with him so he could sit next to a friend of his. I agreed readily enough – only to discover the real reason for him wanting to change places was that the desk I was now sitting at was collapsing.

I took the whole exam concentrating more on holding up the desk with my knee than on the subject. I was too shy to inform the teacher in charge of the exam!

I knew I had not done well, but fortunately I had done well enough to get through. In fact I got my first job – on the Knutsford Guardian – before I knew whether I had passed or not and by the time I got my result I had been working for several months.

You might think I would have no further contact with Jimmy or Knutsford College. But in fact, Neville Kaye and I would go on many walks in the fields around Woodside, with his lovely Golden Retriever, Susie, so we often passed the entrance to the school and noted some of the changes taking place. The conversion of various rooms from classrooms and dormitories to flats was not apparent from outside, of course, but the grounds were soon full of caravans which Jimmy had made and then let

I don't know how many people lived on the site, but it was enough for Jimmy and his wife to live on the rental income.

Jimmy would also hire out his car and was a frequent visitor to the Guardian office to place small advertisements for "car hire" or "flats to let."

I often saw him at the office and found I was still calling him "Sir." Whether or not he felt any sense of pride in seeing one of his former students working on the local newspaper, I can only guess. But in fact, getting the job had more to do with me having a father who was a journalist than with my education at Knutsford College, Grimes' College or with my GCSE O Level results.

A condition of my employment was that I owned a bicycle to enable me to get around the Knutsford area and outlying villages such as Mobberley, Ollerton, Chelford, Over Peover, Lower Peover and Mere.

I should mention here that because of what I now realise was their firm belief that I needed to be sheltered, my parents had never allowed me to have a bicycle and for many years I couldn't even ride one. However, I usually came home from school with Bob Jackson, who did have a bike and over a period of time he taught me the basics of cycling.

So in the week before I started at the Guardian, my father took me to Harry Elstone's cycle shop in Princess Street and bought me a brand new, bright red, Dayton Flyer for what seemed to me the princely sum of 18 guineas.

Cycling around Knutsford and district, including perilous journeys along unlit country lanes, to attend parish council meetings on dark, winter nights, soon made me a proficient cyclist.

In the fullness of time, I began to make more friends around Knutsford – some of who became members of our unofficial club in the barn. From within the club membership a small group emerged whose main interest in life at that time was the pursuit of the opposite sex. Bob and I, and on occasions, Martin Moore, were the only former Knutsford College students involved.

Martin was by this time in the RAF, but when on leave he would return to Knutsford and stay with his step-father and mother - Jimmy and his wife – at Woodside.

In the early 1950s, few young lads possessed a car. I certainly didn't – in fact even my father didn't, although he always maintained the reason for this was not financial but because he suffered from occasional dizzy attacks. If he had one while at the wheel the consequences could be

THE NO HOPER

disastrous, he said, and it seemed a reasonable enough argument. Certainly he did suffer from dizzy attacks because I remember him being brought home by car once after suffering an attack at work.

Anyway, it always seemed to those of us who didn't have a car, that we were at a distinct disadvantage with the opposite sex, compared with those who did have a car – or even a van or a motor cycle. My shiny new Dayton Flyer certainly didn't seem to "pull the birds."

If we wanted to cast our net beyond Knutsford in our search for suitable, or indeed "unsuitable", young ladies, we had to rely on public transport. The last bus or train from the nearest larger towns, such as Altrincham, Macclesfield or Northwich, was usually around 11pm. The last train from Manchester was even earlier and even in the days before all-night clubbing, this was considered pretty early.

Any of our group who was unable to tear himself away from some young lady would inevitably end up hitch-hiking home. If he was unlucky, he might have to walk all the way!

So the arrival back in town of Martin Moore was something of a fillip.

I have already mentioned that Jimmy was now letting his car out to boost his income, but of course when Martin was home, he could obtain the use of the car for free. He could also drive.

This opened up new horizons. We didn't venture much further afield, but at least we knew we would not be walking home.

When Martin was not at home, we decided we would hire the car as Jimmy only charged us 10 shillings. I usually negotiated the deal, but Bob drove as he was the only one among us with a driving licence.

I have to admit I was a little worried when, the first time I telephoned Jimmy to officially book the car, he readily agreed but added: "If anyone asks you, say I have loaned it to you."

I was even more worried when, one night, the steering wheel came off in Bob's hands and he had to show considerable skill to keep the car on the road and bring it to a halt.

THE NO HOPER

He had to drive the car using the spokes in the steering wheel for the rest of the evening.
Generally speaking, the car was not in very good condition. I'll swear it was the same old Austin that was being used to take boys to sing in the choir at Rostherne Church before I even started at the school.

THE FIRST KISS

Although Knutsford College had knocked most of the shyness out of me when it came to dealing with boys, it was a different story when it came to girls. Five years at a boys-only school meant I had had little contact with the opposite sex.

It didn't seem to cause other students any problems. Boarders were always meeting local girls outside the Marcliff Cinema on Saturdays. There was also much talk of liaisons with girls in the Bottom Path. In later life, Michael Bishop, a jazz fan, attended a concert, took a fancy to the singer with the band and ended up marrying her. I call that pretty cool.

Farmer's son Stan Gerrard met his future wife by the simple process of retrieving her hat when it blew off on a windy day and went sailing across a field where he was working. I didn't seem to have that sort of luck!

As a small boy, I don't think I was unusual in disliking little girls. They had squeaky voices, long hair, tended to be noisy and seemed to me to be very bossy. And they played with dolls.

One early traumatic experience probably shaped my view of the female sex for years to come. My mother and I were invited out for tea at one of her friends' homes and when we arrived I discovered a little monster named Maureen lived there. While our mothers chatted, we were expected to play together – and that meant dolls.

Eventually the lady of the house announced that tea was ready and told her daughter: "Show David where the bathroom is and both of you wash your hands."

Maureen took this instruction very seriously. Not only did she show me where the bathroom was, she proceeded to wash me and I was daft enough to let her.

On the way home, my mother asked me: "How did you get on with Maureen?"

I replied dourly: "She scrubbed my face with a scrubbing brush."

THE NO HOPER

For some reason my mother found this amusing and repeated the story over and over to all her friends, much to my embarrassment.

Fast forward a decade or so to my arrival at the Knutsford Guardian with my shiny new bicycle.

Although it was primarily intended for work, it obviously enabled me to get around much more – bringing within range Pickmere Lake, which was about five miles away.

Many of my friends had been cycling there on Saturday afternoons for some time while I was playing cricket for Knutsford 2nd XI. In those days there was a permanent funfair on the lake side, owned and operated by the family of a Knutsford College Old Boy, Brian Cheetham.

Fine fellow though he was, Brian was not the principal attraction at Pickmere – it was girls. They gathered there in large numbers, many travelling by the same mode of transport as my friends – the pedal cycle.

Freed from the responsibility of representing Knutsford on the cricket field and now equipped with my Dayton Flyer, I was able to join this group.

Brian soon showed the value of knowing people in high places. When he was around, I frequently got free rides on the dodgems or in rowing boats on the lake. He and I had known one another for many years because he had also been at Yorston Lodge during part of the time I was there.

But of course, he could not help me with the girls.

It seemed an awful long time before it happened but eventually, one sunny afternoon by the lake I met a girl who, while she was not Jean Simmons, wasn't at all bad.

I bought her an ice cream and we wandered hand-in-hand around the lake, far from the madding crowd, and eventually found a spot in a field overlooking the gently rippling water. I gallantly laid my jacket on the grass for her to sit on and we sat and talked.

Eventually she lay back beside me and I looked down on her, our eyes lingering on each other. The sky was a perfect blue with just a scattering of fluffy white clouds. The sun cast warm red reflections on the lake and high above a skylark wheeled and turned.

THE NO HOPER

Tiny insects buzzed around the wildflowers in the meadowland around us. This was it, I thought. This was what they meant by the birds and the bees. I looked down and saw she was breathing heavily, her lips slightly apart, just waiting to be kissed. Slowly I lowered my head towards hers...
The poor girl probably wondered for months afterwards why that big dopey lad she met at Pickmere didn't kiss her. But in the final moment as our lips were about to meet, I spotted a large, black crow dangling precariously in her left nostril. I was too polite to tell her and too squeamish to kiss her in case it became detached and transferred itself to me.

SERVING MY COUNTRY

While not directly connected to Knutsford College, there was another episode in my life which, when I recount the story to others, is usually greeted either with laughter or with outright disbelief.

When I started at the Knutsford Guardian, one of my regular jobs was to report on the weekly matches of Knutsford Football Club, who played then, as they still do today, in Manchester Road.

This kept me in touch with Geoff Aldridge who used to take his girl friend to watch Knutsford play every Saturday. We college boys really knew how to treat a lady!

I was always pleased to see him because he knew a lot more about football than I did and I would pick his brain to help me write my report. All this ended when he was called up by the RAF and I had to find someone else to teach me the finer points of the game. It also meant the time when I would receive my own letter from the Ministry of Defence was drawing closer.

Quite frankly, I did not want to do National Service at all, partly because I thought it would interfere with my career in journalism but mostly because the idea of two years in the forces terrified me. But if I had to do it, I wanted it to be in the RAF rather than the Army.

My father had served in the RAF, briefly, during the War and Geoff told me I would almost certainly be accepted if I made this known when I was interviewed following my medical.

What he didn't know, of course, was that I was hoping I wouldn't pass the damned medical.

I was pinning my hopes on a pair of in-growing toenails which had developed shortly after I had started work. They were really painful and at times I could barely walk. If it hadn't been for my new bicycle I wouldn't have been much good as a roving reporter.

THE NO HOPER

Eventually I went to see my GP who, after one look at my toes, arranged for me to be admitted to Knutsford Cottage Hospital to have the nails removed.

In those days, this involved quite a nasty operation, under general anaesthetic, to have the whole nail taken out. Afterwards, I had to have a week in hospital where a sadistic nurse seemed to take great pleasure in changing the dressing on my raw and bloodied toes every day. There were guys in the ward for much more serious operations who, when they saw the treatment I was getting, confessed they would not want to swap places with me.

Anyway, I went back to work and in the fullness of time, my toenails grew again. And guess what? They soon became just as bad as before and, by the time my National Service medical came around, resembled two pieces of raw meat. I was elated – surely I would now be judged unfit for military service!

I went into Manchester for the medical which involved stripping off and being poked and prodded by various men in white coats, who may or may not have been doctors, completing some sort of IQ test, which seemed a complete nonsense to me, and at some stage being asked by an officer why I wanted to join the RAF.

Remembering what Geoff Aldridge had told me, my reply was: "Because my father served before me, Sir."

I didn't mention that he had only served for nine months and had been invalided out after suffering dizzy attacks during training.

There seemed to me to be a lot of emphasis being put on sport. What sports did I play? At what level did I play? Had I ever played any sport professionally? For once, I kept quiet about cricket. In the circumstances, I would, wouldn't I? I was still hoping I would fail the medical so the more unfit I could make myself seem the better

In any case I had been forced to give cricket up when I started work because I had to attend shorthand and typing classes on Tuesdays and

THE NO HOPER

Thursdays which were also net practice nights at the club. Players who did not attend net practise tended not to get selected.

Anyway, the shorthand and typing classes seemed quite attractive at the time. I had spent most of my school years in an all-boys establishment and now I was the only boy in a class of about 30 girls!

I have often wondered whether this is why I was never much good at shorthand.

Eventually, the medical and subsequent interrogation ended and I was ushered into an office where a friendly looking officer looked up from a pile of papers on his desk, smiled and said: "Congratulations – you have passed as Grade 2, which means you are suitable for the RAF."

I tried to look pleased, in case he changed his mind and put me in the Army. But really I was devastated. All that effort put into getting unfit had been in vain.

Well, of course there was a wait of several months before I received my call-up papers informing me of the date I was to report for induction and initial training at RAF Cardington, Bedfordshire. Provisionally, it had been decided I should train as a court shorthand writer.

After that, the time seemed to fly by too damn quickly. Before I knew it I was in my last week at work – and the staff were presenting me with a pen and pencil set as a parting gift.

My job was safe, of course. I knew I would be taken back – there was just the little matter of two years in the RAF to endure in the meantime.

I was quite agreeably surprised when I got to Cardington. I had met another new recruit on the train who was just as terrified as me and that made me feel better.

The corporal who greeted us – and about 30 others on the same train – seemed a pleasant enough fellow, which was not what I had expected after hearing my father's stories about corporals he had come up against. I had expected someone who would make even Percy seem as gentle as a lamb.

We were marched to a hut with about 40 beds in it and then, to my horror, the friendly corporal pointed at me and said: "I'm appointing you senior hut man – that means if this hut isn't kept in good order, you get the blame."

The corporal was known as a marshal – and that led to me being dubbed "the sheriff" by the other recruits.

Of course, the corporal couldn't have picked a worse person than me to take charge of a hut full of new recruits and over the next few days I had some difficulty to maintaining any sort of order when he was not around. I do remember when the lights went out on the first night, a Cockney voice from the other end of the hut said: "Cor blimey – if this is what it's going to be like, I'm orf over the wall."

Another voice in the darkness responded: "But there ain't no wall."

The Cockney replied: "I'll find a bloody wall to go over."

Everybody laughed – and I went to sleep feeling OK.

My first day and I was in charge of a hut already. At this rate I could be an Air Vice Marshal by the time my two years was up.

The next day we were all given forms to fill in and one of the questions was: "Is there any reason why you should be excused wearing boots?"

I filled it in, sparing no detail but without much hope of anything other than, perhaps, escaping some square bashing.

After a day during which the RAF discovered it did not have any uniforms or boots to fit me, I was summoned to see a medical officer.

"What's this about being excused boots?" he asked. I explained – and removed my shoes and socks so he could examine my toes which, after several days of neglect, were looking pretty horrible.

"Aaaah," he said, after a brief examination. He reached for a form on his desk and started to fill it in. "I'm sending you home."

"What?" I gasped.

"You'll have nothing but trouble with those toes my lad. When you get home, go and see your GP and arrange to have them removed at the first joint. It's the only way you'll cure that problem. You'll have to learn to walk again, but you can manage with half a big toe. I know of professional footballers who have had it done.

THE NO HOPER

"And you won't have any more trouble with the RAF."
Next thing I knew I was being issued with a discharge and a travel warrant to get me back home.
The airman issuing the documents said: "You can catch a train tonight, but it will only get you to Altrincham because you'll miss the connection for the last train to Knutsford. I would recommend you stay overnight and travel tomorrow."
Without hesitation I replied: "I'll go tonight."
He was right. I only got as far as Altrincham and had to walk the rest of the way on the feet that had got me out of two years in the RAF. I arrived home at about 2am and, because I didn't have a key, hammered on the door. My startled parents thought I had deserted!
Next day I went to the Guardian office to ask for my job back – four days after I had left.
I walked into the office and my boss stared at me and, before I could say a word, said: "Good God -- have you got leave already?"
They were so surprised they never asked me to return the pen and pencil set.
I went to see my GP, as the RAF medical officer had suggested, and told him I had been advised to have my toes amputated at the first joint:
My GP's response was: "The man's a mad man!"
A couple of days later I received four days pay from the RAF and a couple of months after that I received an invitation to join the RAF Association.
I didn't have the nerve to accept.
Incidentally, I still suffer with in-growing toenails.

DIDN'T THEY DO WELL?

I have already said something about the many characters who attended Knutsford College and, in doing so, have indicated that many former students did pretty well in their future careers. Anyone attending Old Boys' Association reunions would note that they look a pretty affluent bunch.
The few years I was at the school did not give me the opportunity to meet and learn about more than a handful of the former students. Most of them I never knew.
But here's a few who didn't do too badly – with apologies to many others about who I know nothing.

Stephen Davenport really made a name for himself, both as National Hunt Jockey and as a businessman.
By the age of eight he was riding ponies, hunting and show-jumping. He won his first race in 1962 and in 1963-64 was champion amateur jockey with 32 winners. But he raced as a professional too, finishing fourth in the 1964 Grand National riding Eternal.
He won the 1968 Topham Trophy at Aintree, riding Surcharge for trainer John Barclay.
He retired from the saddle in 1975, having ridden 192 winners and then turned to training show-jumpers and breeding horses. He founded Davenport Stables at Arclid, which is still in business today, run by his son James, also a successful show-jumper.
But if all that was not enough, Stephen also ran a successful tyre retailing business for more than 20 years.

Peter Chadwick – he of the secret den and communications system in the basement – was persuaded to join the Royal Navy after qualifying as a marine radio officer in the Merchant Navy. His divisional officer was one Lt Philip Mountbatten. During the Cold War he was moved to the Joint

THE NO HOPER

Services School for Linguists to learn Russian and served in Denmark "listening in" to radio transmissions in the Baltic and passing them on to the top-secret code-breaking centre at Bletchley Park.
On leaving the Navy he held a number of senior management positions in retailing, in this country, West Africa, the United States, South Africa and Australia before running the Australian Government publishing service.
Incidentally, Peter laid claim to being the last student to live at Woodside. After he left the Royal Navy he obtained a job in Manchester and, having learned that Jimmy had converted the college into flats, rented one for a few months before buying a house in Knutsford. It's a wonder he didn't build another den in the basement!

Mayson Howard Balshaw – who, strangely, looked back on the college as "a fine academic establishment" – became a civil engineer, working in local government and on the Corby New Town project in Northamptonshire. He was also a talented organist and pianist and played as a church organist for many years.

Geoff Lomas founded a racing car company and his cars raced at Brands Hatch and on one occasion took first and second places in a race at Mallory Park. He emigrated to Australia in 1986 and subsequently was asked by the West Australian Federal Government to set up the Australian Rare Breeds Reservation. In his 80s he was still working on the development of a solar powered bicycle which he believed was the future for transportation.

Des Donnelly qualified as an accountant, an honourable profession if ever there was one and in addition to carving out a career for himself, helped numerous charities and voluntary groups to balance their books.

Gerald Pullen worked in the film industry and was involved in designing special effects and models for the 1936 science fiction film "Things to

Come," based on H.G.Wells' novel "The Shape of Things to Come", produced by Alexander Korda and starring Raymond Massey, Edward Chapman, Ralph Richardson, Margaretta Scott, Cedric Hardwicke, Maurice Braddell, Derrick De Marney, and Ann Todd.

Geoff Aldridge joined the family business which dealt in cork and wood products. In 1980 it merged with a company in Singapore and Geoff became sales director, which involved much travel in the UK and the Far East. He was also interested in local government and served as both a parish councillor and a borough councillor.

Edward (Ted) Atkinson served in the Merchant Navy but later became a production manager with Ferranti, the major electrical engineering and defence equipment firm.

Ronnie Paulo came from a circus family, which probably explained why he was often to be seen riding one of Percy's horses bareback around the grounds.
Just what part he played in the colourful history of Paulo's Circus, which dates from 1816 and is one of the oldest circus families in Britain, I do not know.
But I have seen posters advertising the circus in various parts of the country while on holiday and actually stumbled upon its Big Top when it was in the Altrincham area a few years ago.
It was quite early in the morning and there was nobody about other than a bored-looking girl behind a kiosk who looked at me as if I was a second-hand car salesman when I enquired if there was a Mr Paulo about. Yes there was, but he wasn't here just now. No, she hadn't heard of a Mr Ronald Paulo. But if I would like to buy a ticket for the afternoon performance...
As recently as 2020 I discovered that Paulo's Circus was still going, despite several setbacks which could have led to its closure and was about

THE NO HOPER

to launch the UK's first drive-in circus. Sounds like it is adapting well to the changing world in which we now live.

I subsequently learned that Ronnie had married a trapeze artist and had retired.

Another Old Boy with show business connections was Brian Cheetham – already mentioned for his connections with Pickmere Lake. His family ran the funfair and pleasure boat company on the banks of Pickmere Lake, about five miles from Knutsford, for more than 60 years.

The Cheetham family carried on running the fair until 1990 when they retired. The new owners, apparently, never made a go of it and the fairground closed, probably to the relief of nearby residents, who would have had to put up with loud music and hundreds of day trippers every weekend.

According to Pickmere Parish Council the rowing boats and small motor boats fell into disrepair and big cruise launch, Princess Irene, which used to take visitors on trips, was sunk in the middle of the lake.

Some years ago I took my granddaughters to see where I used to go all those years ago and found the lake as beautiful as ever, but with no trace of the fairground. A nearby resident told us she was always meeting people making nostalgic trips back to the area in search of the place where they had spent many happy days in their youth.

I wondered whether the girl I never kissed was one of them.

Robert Brunt was something of a legend at Knutsford College – as being one of the few students to ever come to school on horseback.

He would leave the horse in one of Percy's fields, off Manor Park Drive, do a day's work in the classroom and then ride home again in the evening.

Home was Sudlow Farm, Tabley, which is where the stray "doodlebug" which flew over my home ended up. The farm eventually became famous as one of the first fruit farms in Cheshire, specialising in pick-your-own strawberries.

THE NO HOPER

This was all down to Robert who took over running the farm when he was just 19, following the death of his father, Samuel, and swiftly became a highly successful businessman.

He had just joined the RAF and had to return to the family business after only three days as farming was a reserved occupation at that time. His RAF career was, therefore, even shorter than mine – but it has to be said that his escape from military service was a good deal more honourable than mine.

Sudlow Farm was originally a dairy and arable farm but Robert eventually took a chance and branched out into fruit farming. As a pick-your-own enterprise it became regionally famous. At its peak, more than 100 people would be picking for the market and hundreds more self-picking.

Eric Warburton was another farmer's son who sometimes travelled to school by horse – a wonderful animal named Horace. I believe, he – Eric that is, not Horace - went on to become a leading figure in agriculture in the North West.

He farmed Dairy House Farm, Ashley and when World War 2 broke out he had evacuees on the farm, soldiers billeted there and even POWs working in the fields. He was part of the drive to keep the country well fed when food reserves fell to a critical level because of the U-boat blockade.

He bought the farm's first tractor and became one of the first in the area to invest in a combine harvester. His love of everything mechanical led to him becoming a skilled engineer and also diversifying into contracting, carrying out work on the development of the new town of Wythenshawe.

He had a love of quality cars and over the years owned a Humber Super Snipe, two Bentleys and a Jenson.

Peter Wright modestly says "I was just a milkman." But in fact he was an astute businessman who ran a successful dairy products company serving the prosperous Hale, Bowdon and Altrincham areas. He sold out at the right time – just before everybody started buying their milk at

THE NO HOPER

supermarkets instead of having it delivered on the doorstep – and then helped his son establish a major garden machinery business at Ashley.
But Peter was also a talented sportsman playing soccer for Broadheath Central in the Mid-Cheshire League, and a top table tennis player, eventually becoming president of the Altrincham and District Table Tennis League.
He also played squash at Bowdon and was a founder of the Silver Feather Badminton Club, one of the leading clubs in the area.
He told me: "I have had a fantastic life. Never wanted for anything."

Brian Newton stayed at Knutsford College until it closed, moving to Knutsford High School and eventually becoming Head Boy there. He qualified as a mechanical engineer and his work took him to the United States, Russia and Italy.
Later he bought a farm at Coppull, Lancashire as well as working for Bolton Corporation as director of building maintenance.
He then had a complete change of career, gaining a degree in psychology, lecturing at Bolton University, working in the NHS and also setting up his own private practise.
In his spare time he played the cornet – at one time as a member of Knutsford Silver Band – and also obtained his pilot's licence as a member of Lancashire Aero Club.

Ian Duncan became a professional golfer – his father George had captained the Ryder Cup team in 1929 when they regained the trophy from the United States. Ian held positions at Mere Golf Club, near Knutsford and Alwoodley Golf Club, near Leeds before retiring as a full-time professional in 1996.

John Partingtion, better known at Knutsford College as "JD" had the reputation of being one of the best known and remembered student in the school's 27-year history.

THE NO HOPER

He was a fine all round sportsman, football, horse riding and, particularly cricket so I imagine he and I would have got on well had we both been there at the same time. He came from a cricketing family and it's believed that at one time there was a Partington XI. Wherever he moved – and that was far and wide – he played for the local cricket club.
He served in the Royal Navy and on his return to civilian life worked in Africa – East and West – in what he described as the "rag trade" and also becoming a part-time jockey before returning to this country to pursue a successful business career and carry on playing cricket until he was over 70.

Len Williams' first job after leaving Knutsford College was as a teacher...at Knutsford College. Percy let him stay on because of the lack of jobs due to the looming clouds of war in Europe.
But later he worked in the aviation industry building the Handley Page Halifax and the Lancaster bomber for the war effort. After the war he studied to become an analytical chemist, becoming a Member of the Royal Institute of Chemists.

Brothers Adam and Frank Lythgoe both had successful business careers and were associated with agricultural chemicals manufacturing firm Adam Lythgoe. Frank was also a farmer and a well-known traction engine enthusiast. For many years he kept up a tradition of driving one of his steam engines around the Lymm and Warburton areas where he lived on Christmas Day morning.

Geoff Holmes, together with John White, was largely responsible for founding the Old Boys' association, still functioning more than 60 years after the college closed.
Early annual reunions in the 1970s were held either at the Legh Arms – Percy and Jimmy's old watering hole - or Cottons Hotel, Knutsford where

THE NO HOPER

two black-tie dinner dances were held. More recent reunions have been hot pot suppers or pub lunches.
Geoff has acted as the main organising secretary throughout the whole period.

Cliff Eden owned Eden's garage at Mobberley for many years and, in fact, supplied and serviced the Armstrong Siddeley and Austin cars which Percy and Jimmy ran.
He eventually sold out and the garage was demolished and the site redeveloped for housing. But his name lives on as the development is known as Eden Court.

Ian Bleasedale moved to live in the Isle of Man but fell in love with the Greek island of Paxos after holidaying there with his wife, Elizabeth in 1983.
He returned there many times, not just for holidays but also to map the island and produce a guidebook in 1995. He subsequently produced 12 more editions with total sales of more than 50,000. He also wrote a book "Sailing to Paxos and Thereafter" which is available from Amazon.

Doug Griffiths served in the RAF for more than 20 years, during which time he worked as a flight engineer on various aircraft and on the THOR ballistic missile, which included three months in the US.
An early experience was dismantling 20 Spitfires which had been stored since the war.
He said: "Of course I kept many parts for years in my Mum's garage but after finding no use for them I contacted the 'Battle of Britain Flight' who nearly snapped my hand off."
After leaving the RAF he worked with British Caledonian Airways, British Airways and Virgin Atlantic. He did many 13-hour return flights which were nearly always night flights.

THE NO HOPER

"They were a killer – but I don't think they did me too much harm" he said.
Doug, of course, has played a leading role in the Old Boys' Association and created the wonderful website which has done so much to keep the association going. He has carried out hours of research and travelled thousands of miles tracking down long-lost Old Boys and persuading them to attend the annual reunion.

I didn't need to ask Joe Ashley about his long and distinguished career in agriculture - I heard him interviewed about it on BBC Radio Four some years ago.
After working on his Dad's farm at Plumley, Joe - then aged 21 - took part in a Government-backed scheme to revive a rundown nursery near Cambridge. He was there for 20 years, selling top quality produce to the likes of Marks and Spencer and Sainsbury's before moving on to turn around a failing beef and arable farm near Lowestoft where he stayed for 26 years. You don't get on Radio Four for nothing!
In addition to that - and I'm sure you'll expect me to mention this - he played cricket as a wicketkeeper-batsman until he was 76.

John Gresty arrived at Knutsford College in September 1948 as a 10-year- old full time boarder. In his own words he was "academically less than average."
He did however enjoy two activities ....looking after and riding Percy's horses and woodwork classes with Jimmy.
In December 1951 he moved to the newly formed North Cestrian Grammar School in Altrincham where he excelled. After four years he left, aged 17, as School Captain.
He joined Linotype and Machinery Ltd in Broadheath as a junior photographic assistant and after a four year apprenticeship became a fully trained senior photographer and virtually ran the department. However,

THE NO HOPER

still photography did not fulfil his ambitions so in 1960 he joined Cinephoto Film Productions Ltd in Salford and became the production director.

In a career spanning nearly 40 years he produced more than 200 16mm industrial documentaries - the equivalent of today's corporate videos – his work taking him all over Europe but also to America, Oman, Tanzania and Indonesia. He was even asked to go Hollywood to make two films for an American company! His many clients included ICI, Renold Chains, Fairclough Civil Engineering (now Amec) and Balfour Beatty International Construction.

On his "retirement" he joined his son's company ASG Services Ltd as financial director. He now makes bird and hedgehog boxes and looks after the hive equipment of one of the largest beekeepers in the North West, making good use of the woodworking skills he acquired at Knutsford College.

In a sense, Michael Ball followed in his mother's footsteps – but in a rather different way. She was a master baker with her own business in Warrington – he joined the Royal Navy in the catering branch. He served on cruisers, aircraft carriers and submarines – including nuclear submarines under the northern ice cap, playing cat-and-mouse with Russian submarines. I believe the crews never knew where they were, or even where they had been. So when Mike returned home and was asked "Where have you been?" he would reply: "I've no idea." Later he transferred to a frigate and was involved in the 1972-73 "Cod War". On one occasion his ship was rammed by an Icelandic gunboat and the hull was ripped open.

In 1974 he was involved in the evacuation of British and American forces from Saigon and his ship was the last one out as the city fell to the North Vietnamese.

THE NO HOPER

He retired from the Navy after 24 years but took his reputation with him, becoming head of catering at Kings College, Wimbledon and later Malvern College and Hereford Cathedral before being approached by the Ministry of Defence to take charge of catering at several R.A.F. bases.

Mike, incidentally, started at Knutsford College when he was only four and, as such, is believed to have been the youngest-ever pupil.

THE FINAL YEARS

Jimmy's final years were not happy ones. He had come to rely heavily on his wife, Valerie, and when she left him, some time after the school had closed, he was devastated. He pleaded with her to return but she would not. Eventually, she re-married and left the area. Jimmy lived alone in one of the flats and, on the occasions I saw him, looked a pathetic figure.

He died alone on Leap Year's Day 1960 and his body was found by one of his tenants. He was slumped in a chair surrounded by empty bottles and there was a pile of coal in the room, next to the fireplace, presumably so that he could keep his fire burning without having to go outside for fuel.

It fell to me to cover his inquest when the full details of his tragic death were spelled out to the coroner.

Even after his death, I still found myself wanting to respect his memory. I think this must have been reflected in my report and resulted in me omitting most of the more graphic details.

Jimmy and Percy in happier times

THE NO HOPER

Another journalist, representing another newspaper, was present and he had no such compunctions in reporting the whole sorry story in great detail.

After the reports – his and mine – appeared, a local businessman stopped me in the street and congratulated me on my report.

He said he had known Jimmy well and was saddened by the manner of his passing. He had read both reports and clearly thought the other journalist had exaggerated the story in the interest of selling more newspapers. But really he hadn't – he told it the way it was.

My report in the Knutsford Guardian read as follows:

Death of former headmaster

A verdict of death due to chronic alcoholism was recorded at an inquest at Knutsford on Friday on former Knutsford headmaster Mr James Hope, of Woodside, who was found dead at his home the previous Monday.

Mr Peter Roderick Moore, 27, Meade Close, Knutsford, Mr Hope's stepson, said his step-father had been treated for some years for a liver complaint.

Evidence of finding Mr Hope dead in his room was given by Mrs Muriel Lizard, a tenant at Woodside.

Dr Lionel Phillips said Mr Hope had died of a liver complaint.

"Had there been no history of drinking he might well have been alive today," he added.

The great American novelist F. Scott Fitzgerald once said: "Show me a hero and I will write you a tragedy."

I feel these words are quite appropriate here. My teachers, for all their faults, were my heroes – Percy, Jimmy and, in particular, Denis.

All three died in tragic circumstances.

THE NO HOPER

ANOTHER COLLEGE

There is, of course, another Knutsford College. Haven't I mentioned that? Well there's a good reason for that – when I started writing this book I didn't know about it myself.

I'm not talking about Knutsford Academy, in Bexton Road, formerly known as Knutsford High School and the successor to the very school my parents went to such great pains not to send me to all those years ago. The unwary internet surfer searching for Knutsford College might be directed there, but that is not the one I am talking about.

I'm referring to Knutsford (University) College in Accra, capital city of the Republic of Ghana.

Why the hell a university in West Africa should be named after a small Cheshire town I have been unable to establish. It's true that part of Ghana was, as The Gold Coast, a British Crown Colony, so it is possible there could be some historical connection with Knutsford. It's also true that Lord Maurice Egerton, fourth baron of Tatton, had an estate in Africa and established an agricultural college there, which is now known as Egerton University. But that is in Kenya – almost as far away from Accra as Knutsford.

King Canute – who ruled England, Denmark and Norway - clearly got around a bit but there is no evidence that he had even heard of Africa, never mind been there.

A couple of Old Boys – Peter Chadwick and John Partington – spent some time working in Ghana, but neither of them have laid claim to any actions while there which might result in a college being named after their former school.

Jimmy's theory that the name Knutsford was derived from some guy named Knott owning a ford across a river is, I suppose, even less plausible in West Africa than in North West England. So, for the time being, this little conundrum must remain unsolved. But I am working on it.

However, it is very much a fact that Knutsford (University) College, Accra was established in 2007 as an independent institution to help meet the increasing demands for quality but affordable university education in Ghana, Africa, and across the world.

Not much different, you might think, to Percy Hope's aims when he opened his college in Cheshire in 1927, although I don't recall the word "affordable" cropping up in Percy's prospectus.

The Ghanaian institution is also popularly known as "The Royal University of Africa" – a little surprising in a republic – but clearly deemed appropriate in view of its two "posh" campuses (their words, not mine) and the fact that it is affiliated with the University of Ghana, the nation's premier university.

Knutsford (University) College had just 25 students in 2008 but now has several thousand and has graduated more than 1,000 students. It is now also affiliated with the University for Development Studies, also in Ghana.

Its website states: "Knutsford University College is exceptional. It is mandated to groom, transform, and inspire students to lead godly and purposeful lives, serve society with distinction and integrity, and passionately enrich lives everywhere in the world. Therefore our degrees and programmes aim at developing permanent foundations for inspiring leadership and stewardship among our students and graduates for their own personal, intellectual and professional development and as a consequence, for national, international and global development.

"The university recognises the fact that whilst each person must contribute his or her portion for self, communal, national, and global development, leadership is key to a paradigm shift and for fundamental change in every community. Just as people perish with ignorance so do they perish with shortsighted or weak leadership.

"Naturally then, not everyone is a leader and not every programme leads to successful leadership. Leadership can and must be nurtured from among those with demonstrated potential. To ensure creative, active, wise, disciplined and inspiring leadership amongst our students, therefore, at Knutsford the subject of leadership is central to our programmes and is consciously developed as a specific, comprehensive, and detailed programme of character building and heroic thinking."

Again, this is not much different to Percy's avowed intention in 1927 of "uplifting of character so that the boys could live their lives in the fulfilment of duty, rather than as a means of gaining worldly advancement alone."

Knutsford (University} College is currently developing four academic schools: Knutsford Business School (KBS), Knutsford School of Humanities and Education (KSHE), Knutsford School of Science and Technology (KSST), and Knutsford School of Graduate Studies and Research (KSGSR) so appears to have a bright future.

AND FINALLY

Well, there you have it. I have spilled the beans on Knutsford College, almost 70 years after it closed.

The questions remain: Were my parents right in deciding I was a No Hoper and did they do the right thing in sending me to Percy Hope's school for the sons of gentlemen?

I'm sure there were other pretty hopeless cases who attended the school over the years, although the reader will surely have gathered by now that for most of the time I did not consider any of them to be as hopeless as me. Certainly few could have had such an inauspicious introduction to the school as I.

But most left well equipped to face the world, whether or not they had arrived as No Hopers.

Was I a No Hoper? Well, on the one hand, I was thrown head first through a holly bush. I turned up for drill wearing a raincoat. I acquired the nickname "Skentelbollocks" and was, for a time, the laughing stock of the school. I suffered some kind of nervous breakdown because I was terrified of the maths teacher. And it was me in goal when the school football team lost 8-0. I left the school with nothing other than a table tennis table.

I served my country in the RAF – for four days, including travelling! I missed out on my first kiss because of a crow.

On the other hand...well it shouldn't be left to me to put the opposite argument. But I will anyway because no-one else will.

First and foremost I met a beautiful girl, Patricia and, incredibly, persuaded her to marry me. An astute businesswoman, she ran her own town centre art and craft shop for many years and then came into my business to revolutionise the accounts department.

Together we produced a fine son, Gary, who, with his wife, Janet, presented us with two beautiful granddaughters, Amy, who recently

THE NO HOPER

obtained her M.A. and Hannah who has joined the family business and presented us with a beautiful great granddaughter, Olivia.

Until we downsized, Patricia and I lived in a 300-year-old house at Lymm, Cheshire which, if we wanted to buy it back today, would probably cost us more than £1 million.

No-Hoper or not, I think I did pretty well.

But in addition I captained the school cricket team. You'd expect me to mention that, wouldn't you? I published the school magazine and I wrote an essay which predicted acid rain years before it arrived. I'd forgotten that until Brian Newton reminded me of it at an Old Boys' reunion!

After leaving school I trained as a journalist on the Knutsford Guardian. Briefly I was chief reporter on the Warrington Guardian before moving to the Lancashire Evening Post where for about 10 years I wrote a weekly column in which I said nasty things about almost everybody and everything. In the space of one 12 month period I was accused of being unfair by all three main political parties, so I reckon I must have been doing something right.

I founded a news and publishing business which is still going after more than 50 years, thanks to Gary, who has moved it forward, embracing all the wonders of modern technology.

Although I had to give up playing cricket when I started work, I returned to the game when I was nearly 40, playing for three different clubs, Glazebury, Lymm Oughtrington Park and Capenhurst, until finally hanging up my bat at 77 – years, that is, not runs.

In that time I scored 4,932 runs at an average of 14.2 and took 33 wickets rather expensively. Not too many club cricketers would have kept such a detailed record over so many years.

But then I would, wouldn't I?

No Hoper? My arse!

ALUMNI

There is no accurate record of how many students passed through the portals of Knutsford College in its 27 year history but a rough, back-of-an envelope calculation suggests it could be around 1,350. The following list is far from complete, although its existence represents an astounding piece of research by Doug Griffiths, owner and editor of the website www.knutsfordcollege.com. If any reader should find that they, or a relative or acquaintance, is missing from the list, please let Doug know.

This book indicates that many Old Boys did pretty well for themselves in later life, but I can say little more than that. As far as I know there were no prime ministers, bishops or mass murderers.

The following list is of students Doug Griffiths has managed to trace, although the dates indicated suggest that a few may have attended one of Percy Hope's earlier schools – possibly moving with him when he moved the school. Sadly, but inevitably, the majority have passed on.

Adshead, Ted (1946-1949); Aldridge, Geoffrey (1942-1952); Aldridge, Richard (1942-1948); Andrew, Derek (1939-44); Andrew, Kenneth (1937-1942); Armstrong, David (around 1949); Arrowsmith, Derek (1951-1953); Ashley, Joe (1943-1954); Ashley, Mark (1943-1949; Aspey, W (1949-1951); Aspinal, John (1928-1933); Atkins, John (1948-1950); Atkinson, Edward (1946-1950); Austin, Ken (Around 1937).

THE NO HOPER

Baker, Alex (1929-1935); Baker, John (1945-1951); Ball, Michael (1950-1953); Balshaw (Mayson Howard) 1935-41); Banfield, Tony (1952-1954); Barber, Ian (Around 1940); Barlow, John (1947-1948); Barnes, ? (1942-1946; Bate, David (1949-54); Battersby, A (1951-1954); Beddow, Derrick (1945-1947); Bell, Brian (1942-1947); Bishop, Michael (1946-1951); Black, Michael (1945-1948); Bland, Gilbert (1945-51); Bland, Julian (1949-1954); Bleasdale, Ian (1941-1947); Blockley, Bob (191943-1947); Blockley, George (1940-45); Blockley, John (1938-1943); Bloor, Stephen (1946-1950); Bowe, Brian (1945-1950); Bowler, Arthur (1928-1932); Bowler, Bill (1929-

1933); Bradshaw, Roy (around 1938); Brighouse, Antony (1949-1953); Brighouse, Brian (1951-1954), Broadbent, Frederick (1946-1948); Brocklehurst, Joe (1927-1932); Brocklehurst, Sam (1929-1933); Broughton, Graham (1940 1945); Brunt, Robert (191936-38); Bryning, John (around 1946); Bullivant, Roger (1944-1948); Burgess, B (Around 1949); Burgess, J (around 1950); Burke, Michael (1933-1937); Burke, Victor (1933-1936); Burton, Ken (1929-1934); Butcher, S (1951-54).

Callwood, Harold (1941-1946); Carrington-Walters, Bevis (1951 to 1954); Carter, Donald (1946-1951); Carter, Roland Brian (1944-1948); Carvell, Brian (Around 1949); Chadderton, Geoffrey W (1943-1948); Chadwick, Peter (1941-1948); Challoner, Thomas (1936-1940); Chapman, John (not known); (1928-1932); Chapman, Kenneth Eden (1939-1944); Cheetham, Brian (1944-1949); Childe, J (around 1950); Chorlton, Michael (around 1950) Clark, B - Nobby (around 1949); Clarkson, John (1927-1930); Clarkson, John (1943-1948); Cooke, Paul (1946-48); Cooper, Barry (1947-1951); Cooper, Stanley (1925-1930); Corker, Kenneth (around 1945); Cotterill, John (1946-1951); Cowan, Terry (1944-1948); Coy, Graham (around 1948); Crisp, ? (around 1943); Crosby, Peter (1937-1942); Croxall, Ralph (1949-1951); Cunnellon, Brian (1941-1945); Cunnellon, Peter (1941-1945); Curtis, Roger (1950-1953).

Dakin, Alf (around 1940), Dakin, Geoffrey (unknown); Dakin, Frank (1948-52); Dale, Malcolm (1945-49); Darlington, Albert (1944-1949); Darlington, Tom (1947-52); Davenport, G. Leigh (1944-1947); Davenport, Michael (1951-1953); Davenport, Stephen G. (1951-53); Davey, Harry (1939-1945); Davidson, John (1951-1953); Davis, D. Keith (1944-1948); Dewhurst, Carl (1941-45); Dillon, Mike

THE NO HOPER

(around 1942); Donnelly, Desmond (1944-1945); Duncan, Ian (1928-1934); Dyson, John (1945-1948).

Eaton, Albert (1928-1932); Eaton, Tom (1928-1930); Ebrey, Ronald (1947-1950); Eden, Cliff (1935-38); Eden, George (1933-38); Eden, George Mason (1928-1935); Eden, Stanley (1935-1938); Edgill, Derek (1949-1950); Edwards, Ian (1945-1949); Egerton, John (1946-1950); Escourt, Big (around 1935); Escourt, Little (around 1935).

Fairclough, John (1943-1950); Farley, John (1946-51); Farrah, A (1925-1930); Farrah, E (1925-1930); Farrar (1925-1930); Fleetwood, Mike (1941-46); Frith, Roland (1947-1950); Fryer, David (1941-1947).

Gallimore, John (around 1949); Gallimore, P (around 1937); Gerrard, Alan (1940-45); Gerrard, Stanley (1940-1943); Gibbon, David (1941-47); Gibson, Ronald (around 1940); Goostrey, Leslie (1940-1943); Goostrey, Malcolm (1945-1950); Goostrey, Thomas (1945-1949); Gore, Bob (1940-1944); Gradwell, Donald (1936-1939); Gray, Derek (1942-1945); Greenhalgh, S (not known); Gresty, John M (1949-1951); Griffiths, Douglas (1945-1951); Griffiths, Ronald (1935-1941); Grosvenor, Barry (1948-1953).

Hall, J (not known); Hamley, Vic (not known); Hamman, Peter (1939-1944); Hankinson, Alan (1949-1952); Hankinson, Ted (1946-1949); Hartley, Brian (1937-1942); Harvey, Hugh (1944-1948); Harvey, Ross (1945-1948); Hatton, David (1949-1950); Hayman, Don (1945-1950); Hetherington, Roy (1929-1932).

Jackson, Bob (1942-1946); Jackson, Geoffrey (1945-1950); Jackson, R (!951-1953); Jackson, Sam (1942-1944); Jackson, Terry (1942-1945); Jervis, Joseph Trevor) (1941-1945); Jones, Gethin (1946-1951); Jones, K (around 1950); Jones, Russell (1940-1946).

Kaye, Neville (1944-1952); Kaye, Russell (1935-1940); Kendall, Brian (1932-1938); Kendal, Peter (1935-1940); Kent, Keneth (191946-1948); Kershaw, Peter (1941-1947); Kinsey, John (1929-1934); Kinsey, Michael (1945-1951); Kinsey, Norman (around 1930); Knott, John (1942-1948),

THE NO HOPER

Leach, John (1927-1937); Leech, Bill (1937-1942); Leech, David (1944-1947); Leech, George Ernest (1943-1947); Leech, Kenneth (1936-1943); Leech, Peter (1944-1949); Lees, John Samuel (191942-1949); Leigh, Tom (1929-1932); Lever, John (191941-1947); Lever, John (191941-1947); Lewis, Frank (not known); Lewis, Gary (1951-1954); Lewis, Harvey (1937-1942); Lewis, John M (1944-1949); Lewis, Ken (not known); Linney, Geoffrey (1949-1951); Linney, John (not known); Lomas, Geoffrey (1946-1950); Lomas, Gerald (1941-1946); Lomas, W (1947-1950); Looker, John (1941-1945); Lunt, Rodney (1950-1953); Lynch, Peter (1942-1944); Lythgoe, Adam (1949-1951); Lythgoe, Frank (1949-1951).

Marojulis, Peter (1946-1948); Marsh, Rodney (around 1945); Martin, John (around 1949); Martin, Roger (1941-1943); Martin-Bird, Richard (1946-1947);

Mason, John (1937-1942); Mason, Vince (1935-1939); Mayer, Bill (1939-1940); McNulty, Brian (1949-52); Metcalfe, Michael (around 1940); Molyneux, J (1936-1939); Moore, Gerald (around 1937); Moore, Martin (1946-1954); Moore, Michael (11938-1946); Moore, Rory (1944-1949); Moreton, James Trent (1951-1953); Moreton, John (1946-1950); Moth, Timothy (1950-1953); Mountfield, R (not known); Murray, Pam (1929-1932); Murray, R.J. Patrick (1928-1934).

Newall, Gerald Maurice (1947-1952); Newton, Brian (1945-1951); Newton, Kenneth (1947-1951); Norbury, "Squirt" (around 1935); Norem, Max (not known); Nott, Malcolm (1944-1946).

Oliver, C (around 1949); Oliver, G (around 1949); Osmond, Gerald (1929-1936); Osmond, John (1930-1938); Owen, Geoff (191950-1952).

Painter, Graham (1946-1949); Parker, R (1951-1954); Partington, Frank (around 1938); Partington, John Derek (1937-1944); Patchett, Frank (1949-1951) Patchett, Roger (1949-1951); Paulo, Ronnie (1946-1949); Peach, Vernon (1935-1938); Peacock, Mary (1928-1932); Pearson, Eddie (1942-1948); Pemberton, Charles (1949-1953); Pemberton, Jimmy (around 1949); Pennington, Samuel F (1931-1934); Percival, John (1926-1934); Pierpoint, Syd (1951-1953); Pimlott, Harry (1944-1949); Plant, Michael (1953-1954); Platt, John (around 1946); Price, J (around 1945); Price, Max (1946-1950); Price, R (1946); Prince, Raymond (1940-45); Prince, Trevor (1942-1945); Pullen, Gerald (1928-1934).

THE NO HOPER

Read, Donald (1951-1954); Reece, John (1942-1945); Roberts, John (around 1942); Roberts, Glynne (1947-1950); Roberts, Peter (around 1936); Robinson, Jack (1936-1939); Rogerson, Geoffrey (1944-1948); Royale, John (1945-1948).

Sands, David (1949-1951); Sawyer, Jim (1935-1939); Shaw, Bill (1936-1940); Shawcross, Barry (1948-1951); Sheard, Phillip (1931-1935); Sheard, R (1931-1936); Sheppard, Roy (1935-1938); Sherlock, Fred (1928-1931); Shore, Joe (1944-1948); Simister, Mary (1928-1931); Simpson, Eric (around 1940); Singleton, J (191950-1951); Skentelbery, David (1948-1954); Smith, Karl (1950-1954); Southern, Brian (1949-1951) Southern, Sydney (1939-1941); Stafford, J (1951-1954); Stanier, Joe (1947-1954); Stanier, Wilfred (1929-1933); Steele, Bill (1931-1936); Steele, John (191941-1949); Stockdale, D (1951-1954); Stringer, John (1943-1951); Stubbs, Peter (around 1942); Sturrock, K (around 1937).

Taylor, Barrie (1947-1951); Taylor, Clive (around 1932); Taylor, Donald (1948-1949); Taylor, Frederick (1935-1942), Taylor, Geoffrey (around) 1930); Taylor,

Michael (around 1933); Taylor-Jackson, David (1944-1947); Thompson, Alec (1942-1945); Tomlinson, Geoffrey (194-1951); Townsend, Horace (1927-1931).

Underwood, David (1937-1941); Underwood, Frank (1937-1942).

Vaughan, Raymond (around 1940).

Wainwright, Geoffrey (1947-51); Wainwright, Stanley (1948-1951); Waldron, Clive (around 1949); Waldron, Cyril (around 1949); Waldron, Eric (1927-1933); Walley, Tony (1944-1951); Walters, John (around 1941); Warburton, Eric (1932-1934); Warburton, Harry (191926-1933); Warburton, Jimmy (1935-42); Warburton, John (1930-1937); Warburton, John Kenneth (1932-1934); Warburton, Mary (1928-1932); Wardle, John (1941-1947); Watson, Norman ((1951-1954); Webb, Peter (1947-1951); Webster, ? (around 1942); Westwood, John (1947-50); Whalley, Gilbert (1937-1942); White, John (1946-1951); Whittaker, John (around 1945); Whitworth, Barry (around 1949); Wilcox, Anthony (1950-1953); Wildgoose, John (1950-1954); Wilkinson, George (1943-1948); Willet, David (1951-1954); Willet, Peter (not known); Williams, E "Taffy" (1928-1935) ; Williams, Leonard (1930-1937); Williams, Nigel (1935-

THE NO HOPER

1941); Williamson, Frank Oswald (1938-1944); Wilson, Ronald (1933-1940); Wood, James (1928-1931); Wood, Norman (1941-1946); Woodward, Bob (1942-1945); Woolstencroft, David (1943-1953); Worsley, Raymond (1940-1945); Wright, Billy (1945-1947); Wright, C (around 1940); Wright, Paul (1952-1954); Wright, Peter (1937-1951).

Yarwood, Peter (around 1945); Yee, Charlie (1929-1936); Young, Peter (1937-1941); Young, Tony (around 1942).

Zebedee, Fred (actually, I made that one up!}

ABOUT THE AUTHOR

David Skentelbery has worked as a journalist in the North West of England for more than 60 years after starting his career in Knutsford shortly after leaving school.
His work has appeared in the national and regional press, on radio and television and in numerous magazines.
In 1968 he founded Orbit News Ltd., a news and picture agency based in Warrington and in 1999, together with his son, Gary, launched www.warrington-worldwide.co.uk - the first independent daily internet newspaper in the country.
The company also publishes a number of monthly magazines
In 2007 David published his first book, "Jumbles Wood" - a fantasy for children.
He lives in Cheshire with his wife Patricia

ACKNOWLEDGEMENT

The author would like to acknowledge the help received from various former students of Knutsford College and, in particular, Doug Griffiths, owner and editor of the website www.knutsford-college.com, without whose help this book could not have been written. Also John Samples for allowing the use his fine painting of the college building, and the staff at Knutsford Library

THE NO HOPER

Printed in Great Britain
by Amazon